LADIES START YOUR BUSINESS NOW

A Woman's Guide To Building a Business From The Dream Up

By
Barbee Kinnison

ISBN: 1-4196-9269-0
ISBN-13: 9781419692697

Library of Congress Control Number: 2008902167

PREFACE

Starting and keeping a business running smoothly is hardly ever easy, and even more difficult in today's entrepreneurial environment. This book has been written to help point you in the right direction. Some of you may already be familiar with many of the details of starting up and getting into your own business; still others may never even have imagined some of the situations a businesswoman could find herself involved in.

No matter how simple it may be to start up the particular business you have in mind, it can always be made more difficult by not having the information you need, when you need it. Conversely, having the right information will put you into a totally different "space," and being in the right space can help put you in harmony with the work you are meant to do.

This book is filled with many details and supplemental information, just in case you need one or all of them to help get your dream off the drawing board, into the workplace, and on the road to success.

This book brings thoughts and requirements together, and while some of the sundry information available might overlap and reaffirm the basic premise for "success," good ideas are good ideas, no matter where they are committed on paper.

I hope to have covered everything you ever wanted to know about all that other stuff regarding the business world, and enjoying it once you're there. That last part may be the most important part; happiness doesn't just happen automatically following "success" or there wouldn't be so many unhappy people at the top.

The great thing about being an entrepreneur—your own "boss"—is that there are no rules about what your dream should be and you can change it as you go. You do not have to stay in a job, a career, or a situation that is not working for you. Remember: you are in charge. Do what you desire, and follow your heart to your own level of success.

So, having stated the above, I invite you to read through, savor, and use whatever you find within these pages that apply to you. If I have missed covering something that you wish I had covered, please drop me a line through my Website. I want this book to be the companion guide for women going into business, so women everywhere can recognize their dreams, and can have a starting point, a continuity coach, a source of encouragement, and a reference for those ever-appearing unexpected situations that make life and business so challenging and exciting.

I hope you find that building your business from the dream up is exciting, amply profitable, a little easier than you thought it might be, and, most of all, a source of personal satisfaction and tremendous joy.

TABLE OF CONTENTS

Acknowledgements

Introduction

ACKNOWLEDGEMENTS

I wish to pay special tribute to my dear friend of too many years to count by now, Joseph Paranto, a very busy man who gave time he didn't have to give, but gave from the heart. He was responsible for the editing of this book from its early stages and for fine-tuning my attitude when I needed it most because he believed in the importance of women in business. His intelligence and insight have been invaluable to me.

Thank you to my children, who initially inspired me to begin this seemingly lifelong mountain-climbing task.

INTRODUCTION

I. To Every Woman with a Dream

Although I may never meet you, I hope you will come to think of me as a friend; as another woman who is genuinely interested in your success and in the realization of your dream. We can all work hard and smart, as they say, and eventually enjoy that big success, yet we need to appreciate and even welcome the little successes and their contributions to the big picture along the way.

The complexities of business, the long hours and hard work, will not take such a tough toll on you if you really enjoy what you are doing. It will not be just a job; it will be a vocation full of profitable, rewarding, and fulfilling days, and your dream will stay alive in spite of any setbacks, detours, or not-so-happy surprises.

If anything you read between these covers helps take the fear out of the unknown, reinforces your resolve to learn all you can about whatever could affect your dream, replaces ignorance with information and naiveté with knowledge, then I will be satisfied that all my trials and tribulations in the world of business have been translated into a usable service. This book should be an aid to your endeavor and will:

- Help you realize you have a dream
- Give you a sense of direction and a blueprint for action
- Tell you what is important to know, what you can find out later, and where you can go to find it

- Advise you of things you might not have considered in your new role as entrepreneur
- Tickle your funny bone when you don't expect it, and hopefully when you do
- Give you ideas, suggestions, insights, and inspiration for your personal success
- Give you self-perpetuating encouragement
- Help you to visualize your dream being fulfilled and your business taking shape
- Help you to solve problems, overcome obstacles, and meet challenges
- Give you practical tips for setting up your office, including hiring, supervising, and appreciating your work team
- Suggest ways to get more out of your business once you're in it
- Tell you how to increase your resource pool and how to use the resources you have to your advantage
- Tell you how NOT to get caught up in the woman-man thing, or the man-woman thing
- Clue you in on some typical business terms and computer jargon; decode some typical business acronyms

- Generally be "your buddy" in the dream-building business

Upon entering the business world nearly thirty years ago, it didn't take me long to see that it was a male-dominated world. Men wanted to talk to and conduct the serious part of the business only with other men. I was treated kindly enough outside of the boardrooms, but once inside, I was treated indifferently and often was completely ignored.

Because I have never been shy and retiring, I was rather surprised and amazed at being treated somewhat like a nonentity in a world that recognized men predominately. As I began to better understand the situation of male dominance—at least in my own industry—I vowed to do what I could to change it. I felt I had worked too hard to allow men to ostracize me in any way. My contributions to the industry were just as valuable and creditable as theirs, and besides, my heart was in my work. I was determined to excel and make my mark. Today I can earnestly say I have enjoyed a formidable career in an industry that was at one time not especially charitable to women. Thank goodness time does change all things.

At some point during those difficult and energy-demanding years, I joined a national businesswoman's organization that held annual conventions and periodic regional seminars in various cities throughout the United States. It was in those meetings and seminars that I seemed to constantly encounter women who had insecurities, or a lack of self-confidence, whether they were already in business or were just thinking about starting one. They came for help and guidance, and of course there was never enough time to give them everything they needed or asked for. I often came away with sad and helpless feelings for some, yet confident and successful feelings for others. What most of them needed was just a little guidance, coupled with a little know-how, tied together with positive reinforcement and encouragement.

When the meetings were over, I began to think of all the women who were not members of such organizations: Women who had no one to meet with, to talk with; no one to be their mentor. Women who were too shy to ask questions. Women who were embarrassed to ask for help because they believed their businesses were too small to be of any concern to a woman with a bigger, more "professional" business. Women who might have so much to offer, and yet would remain silent and afraid, and constantly discouraged. Women who didn't have the luxury of calling their lawyers or accountants for advice because they didn't have lawyers or accountants. Women who didn't want to impose on others, yet were silently crying out for help.

I began to think about my own situation and my past and present business experiences. If only someone had been there for me in the early days, perhaps some of the pitfalls and calamities I encountered could have been avoided. If I could have concentrated more on running and growing a business, instead of having to research and learn so many "I wish I had known that before" kinds of things, I might not have become so entangled in legal and other distracting affairs.

It doesn't take a genius to realize there will always be someone "bigger" and more knowledgeable than yourself in the business world. We will most likely always wish such a person could be there for us, whether it's to answer our questions or just give us a dose of "You can do it, girl!" Heaven knows I needed it! I certainly would have appreciated a listening ear attached to an astute business head guiding me with practical advice.

So, we are on our own, yet most of us would still genuinely appreciate a little help, a "nudge" from anyone who could at least point us in the right direction as we head down the road to where we'd like to be.

II. The Dream Is Born

Within this business pursuit of mine, a thought began to dominate my mind, consuming all my energy and passion, and I just had to put myself "out there" for women struggling to make a go of their own businesses; for women hoping to fulfill their own dreams; for women experiencing that same "nonentity" feeling I had had; for women who just plain don't know what to do or who to ask.

The idea of a book began to take shape in my mind. The contents were beginning to come to me, from the startup to the daily survival to the success. Of course, the "success" part is always a personal thing, and that can only be measured by each individual woman. I knew my experiences, failures, successes, and contributions would prove to be valuable, yet just pondering the undertaking of such a task was overwhelming. I talked myself into and out of the idea many times. The magnitude of the project was staggering!

I discussed my idea with my friends, and they encouraged me to take on the task. In fact, they all loved the idea of a business book particularly for women. Many were so supportive that they put in their orders on the spot! With that kind of encouragement, and my belief in its need, my decision was made.

But, deciding to do something and doing it are two separate things. I started to collect material and information. I did research. I updated my information. I talked to other businesspeople. I made notes. My files were overflowing. I could see the tip of the mountain rising higher and higher—the more I wrote, the more I wanted to add.

I wanted to create a book that would bring together much of the diversified information that can be gotten by wading through countless other books (and there are many good ones out there), attending seminars and workshops (walking on burning coals can do wonders for helping you stand on your own two feet, but that big fee might do more for you if it was spent on your equipment or supplies), paying big bucks for the advice of special consultants (wait until you need them and know exactly who you need), and spending years to learn "the hard way" (ouch!).

I wanted to present a book to women that would offer another woman's personal considerations, insights, possible enlightenment, and the special angle of a woman's view on the world of business.

That's where this book comes in. I've been down a few roads and have had a few adventures, so my task is to help make another woman's journey a little easier. I believe that many women who may otherwise be frustrated at the prospect of tediously wading through yet another business manual, or discouraged at the offerings of yet another expensive, tiresome, or disappointing business workshop (no matter how much fun it might be to meet all those people and play all those games), will find within these pages the clear, concise, useful, and encouraging information they seek, and where to look for more information on a continual basis, because business, like life, is constantly changing as is the electronic age we live in.

I would like to believe that my experiences can save others from the disillusionment often found at the end of yet another go-round on the "trial and error" carousel. And most important of all, I would like to believe that this book can help women avoid some of the unnecessary setbacks and perplexities that rob them of their enthusiasm, their dignity, their time, and eventually even their dream.

This book covers many subjects; some with as little as a sentence or two, some with perhaps more information than you could ever use or want. Some of it may sound as basic as "Don't forget your umbrella," and other parts as esoteric as "The eagle flies at midnight," yet all of it is there for some woman in her own particular circumstances. Although most everyone knows that adventures like jungle safaris, scuba diving, and flying airplanes all have and need a preparation period in which the participants research certain facts in order to ensure the greatest chance of survival, somehow they don't give that much thought to the adventure of <u>business</u>. Preparation is <u>always</u> time well spent. If, for example, you're ever faced with one of those man-eating land sharks out there, it will certainly feel good to know you have options besides being eaten alive.

I also wrote this book to help women avoid some of the particularly annoying, demeaning, and confidence-shaking situations that delay the "construction" of (or, in some cases, even bulldoze) their business before it ever gets off the ground. And finally, to help women recognize, believe in, fine-tune, and get started building the business of their dreams, and to stay encouraged along the way. You know what? Writing this book was my dream!

CHAPTER ONE

DREAMS:
THE WINDOW TO
OUR REAL DESIRES

Dreams Are the Beginning

Somewhere in the vast, exciting, technology driven, and often intimidating world of business, there are women with dreams—dreams of starting their own business. Some of those dreams are delicate and fragile, trying to take root, bud, and get to the threshold of bloom. Likewise, somewhere in this very same world of business there are sneakers and jeans, cardboard files, and coffee cans labeled Petty Cash that are actually taking the initial steps into the world of business, without proper guidance but with plenty of fortitude.

It's been said that behind every successful man, there's a good woman. I think it would be appropriate to mention that behind every successful woman, there is more than likely another successful woman who helped. Before we can be spurred on by anyone's success, it is important for us to know exactly what we are talking about when we speak of being successful.

Success, as defined in the Random House Dictionary of the English Language, is: 1) the favorable or prosperous termination of attempts or endeavors; 2) the attainment of wealth, position, honors, or the like; and 3) a successful performance or achievement. Note that in definition 1), success is found upon the termination of an endeavor; in definition 2), it leaves a lot to the imagination with its all-inclusive use of "or the like," yet it implies attainment of that which others can see, appreciate, or recognize; and in definition 3), it tends to limit success to a particular event, such as graduating from college, singing on stage, or building a house.

As success is spoken of within these pages, you may view it in any one or all of the above-mentioned ways. However, I believe it is very important to view it in yet a different light; a light, in fact, that shines only through the eyes of the woman beholding her own success. What she sees will vary with the nature of her own dream. She may conduct her business in a constant flurry of excitement, and that adrenaline rush is her reward. She may simply believe in herself, and building her business from her dream up is what she must do, for it is the building, not the finished product—the journey, not the destination—that matters most to her. Or, she may, quite frankly, just find she's happiest living, working, and playing in the world of business, whether or not she makes lots of money, gains recognition, or is even considered successful by others.

Personal definitions of success aside—and regardless of all the inspiration and encouragement they may receive—women still need specific answers to their most pressing questions, and workable solutions for their most complicated challenges. Wouldn't it be nice if some kind of guardian angel stood in the wings, waiting to take our hands and lead us to the promised land of success, guiding us around the pitfalls and over the hurdles, through the darkness and into the light? Yet, as we all know far too well, there is no such angel, no such personal prophet proffering professional paradise as we pursue a position of proficiency and profit. (Phew!) And in a way, that's good, because if someone did lead us by the hand, although we might get there faster, it would water down our personal touch and eliminate something that most of us might really want: the challenge!

> *The future belongs to those who believe in the beauty of their dreams.*
>
> -Eleanor Roosevelt
>
> *Some men see things as they are and say why. I dream things that never were and say why not.*
>
> -John F. Kennedy

Your new business adventure must first start with a dream. Your dream may only be an inkling. If so, look for places to help it grow. Any source of material or insight can be used to build on, including this book. Please, don't let anything or anyone:

- Create a dream for you
- Dream the dream for you
- Decide if your particular dream is right for you
- Give you a list of businesses from which to choose and a set of instructions and forms for starting up each particular business

- Do your designing, digging, and building for you
- Climb your stairs or open your doors for you
- Wake you up, keep you going, or put you to sleep at night
- Tell you what to do with your profits
- Guarantee your success
- Envision your end results for you

Pay Attention to Your Joy

We know what we are, but know not what we may be.
    -Shakespeare—*Hamlet*, Act IV, Sec 5

You cannot teach a man anything; you can only help him to find it within himself.
    -Galileo

If you seem to be a little confused about your dream because you're not sure exactly what it is, but you know for sure that you want to be your own boss, have your own business, and somehow contribute something to this world we live in, well...pay attention not only to your talents, skills, and interests, but also to your JOY. When and where are you happiest? Working with what? Working with children? The elderly? Working with numbers? Organizing things around the house? Creating? Fixing? Building? Analyzing? Negotiating?

Researching? Focus on that joy. Imagine getting paid for doing what makes you feel happiest!

List your qualifications for doing this thing, from any kind of experience; learning at your mother's knee, doing it out of necessity, out of desire, for a paycheck, as a volunteer, taking courses, reading books, past hobbies, summer jobs, etc.

Ask your references what they think of your doing such and such as a new career. Then ask them if they would ever use such a service or product, and why or why not.

Keep notes in your "Building My Dream" file. Ask each person in your circle of friends and relatives if they know anyone who can offer any guidance or assistance in that area, and be sure to follow up on it. Pay special attention to how you feel during all this activity. Either you will be inspired with exactly what your dream is, or will find that your particular dream is already underway and requires no further research. One thing you surely will discover, however, is that you need to really have a dream before you can build on it.

None of us know what the outcome will be when we undertake a new venture. We can depend on ourselves for taking care of all the controllable details, we can be spurred on with encouragement from our family and friends, and we can even accept help from strangers—in the form of kind words, advice, or helping hands—yet, in the end, the outcome will be what it will be.

Up until this moment, you've had a life. If it includes a husband or children and you live together, this is a good time to call a family meeting. Tell them what you want to do, why you want to do it, the amount of work you envision it taking, how it will impact on them, the extra help you will need from them, the higher value you will place on your time and, therefore, on the time you will spend with them. Be sure to cover how they feel about what you plan to do. Discuss it until there is understanding and acceptance on all sides.

If we cannot depend on ourselves, who can we depend on? Sometimes, we are all we have. Sometimes, we are fortunate to have something or someone that can help us have the outcome we want. Maybe we would love to once again hear the warm and familiar voice of a mom or dad, a teacher or friend cheering us on, as they did when we were little and had so much to learn. Chances are, this time around those people won't be there—at least not in person. If we can remember a moment of success and the memory of the ones who encouraged and cheered us on, we can forever have that encouragement inside of us.

Dreams and the Future—Moving Forward

If you can imagine it, you can achieve it. If you can dream it, you can become it.
                              -William Arthur Ward

Some men dream of worthy accomplishments, while others stay awake and do them.
                              -Anonymous

I Have A Dream…
                              -Martin Luther King Jr.

Dreams are kind of like doppelgangers, living as they do in two places at the same time. And like doppelgangers, their two selves may look alike, but there is a difference. Today's dreams hopefully will become tomorrow's realities; tomorrow's dreams are always out of reach. It's what we do with today's dreams that makes all the difference.

The words <u>dream</u> and <u>future</u> seem to go together, like "Power Twins." Maybe that's why so many of us spend our time dreaming of the future, without realizing that a little arrives each day. And that's why it's so important to pay attention to each day's worth of our dreams; to use each opportunity, no matter how small or obscure, and each bit of encouragement, no matter the source, to shore us up and spur us on.

When taken in such small portions, our dreams will not overwhelm us. When viewed daily, our opportunities will seem more abundant. And when we seek, accept, expect, and surround ourselves with a daily dose of encouragement, we keep our inspiration, as well as our dreams, alive. Dreaming the dream puts the dreamer—and that's YOU—in that wonderful position of running the show! It's YOUR dream—you can imagine it any way you want it to be!

Unfortunately, some women never give their dreams a chance. Perhaps they've failed at something before, or never even got started, whether held back by fear, habit, or the negativity around them in the guise of well-meaning family or friends. Maybe they just didn't know what to do with their pocket full of seeds, their wheelbarrow full of straw, their bucket full of water...their dreams in the sky.

I would like you to recognize the "hold-back" emotions and/or reasoning, so these don't get a grip on you and keep you from moving forward and building your dream.

The Chains That Bind Us

There are many reasons women hesitate or fail to take the plunge into the world of being in business for themselves. Women are bound and chained by cultural, physical, or circumstantial reasons for holding back and not taking a chance at fulfilling their dreams.

The business world has traditionally been considered a man's world. Women initially entered it to assist men in achieving their goals—as secretaries, typists, researchers, receptionists, assistants, operators, clerks, and the like. Yet, throughout history, certain women have had the courage, the tenacity, and the pioneering spirit to not only believe they had something of their own to offer, but to offer it in spite of the difficulties and the ridicule, and in spite of the idea that "it can't be done."

Nevertheless, women have always been in the world of business, without previously having any of the accompanying titles, benefits, privileges, or paychecks. Such women have been bookkeepers, record keepers, medical care managers, checkbook-balancers, meal and nutrition planners, activities directors, counselors, consultants, mediators, diplomats, saleswomen, buyers, budget-makers, and more. They have been known to successfully negotiate deals in department stores and car dealerships; to reach agreements with teenagers and teachers; to outmaneuver insistent salespeople and solicitors; to screen and interview anyone who has anything to do with their family, from baby-sitters and boyfriends to nudgers and neighbors; and to run a home on a "shoestring and a prayer." Such women have proudly borne the title of "homemaker," "housewife," or "Mom." Yes, today's woman brings a wealth of experience and excitement to the business world. Today's woman can have just as much moxie as any man when she steps into the ring to be her own boss.

- **Lack of Money**
  A chief reason most women will not enter the business arena is due to the fact that we aren't all born rich, marry rich, or attract wealth miraculously. Obviously, if money were no object, many would not want to go into business for themselves, because the main objective is to be financially comfortable with no stress or work. On the other side of the coin, for others money is not the only reward.

- **Other People**
  Those all-too-concerned individuals who are only looking out for your best interests. Their motives may be truly for your personal welfare, or their motives might be subconsciously jealous over your enthusiasm, your success, your idea, your personal change, or any number of other "concerns." If you change for the better, it might mean they would have to change to keep pace with you, share the same level

of excitement with you, or even share the same level of knowledge with you. Some of them just aren't willing to put as much effort into bettering themselves as you are. If they only realized that the joy you impart on others cannot help but return to you, because that is how the laws of the universe operate. That's another subject all its own!

- **Change**
  Change, to many people, is fear of the unknown. It means unfamiliar ground, unfamiliar people, unfamiliar circumstances, unfamiliar tasks, and unfamiliar feelings. Turn this around and look at it as a challenge, an adventure, or a personal advancement gift you give to yourself. Change is good. If change doesn't take place, stagnation—or even worse, complacency—sets in. Everything changes in the course of time. Nothing stays the same, and neither should you.

- **Lack of Self-Confidence**
  This is nothing to be ashamed of. The sober truth is, every person at one time or another has felt this "hold-back" emotion. It is self-imposed as well as imposed by others. We surround ourselves all too often with entirely too many negatives, whether they be in the form of words,

activities, people, or events. One of our biggest handicaps in being women is that we have been raised in an environment to please others above ourselves, as if it is our responsibility. We put our mates first, our children first, our families first, our coworkers first, other businesspeople first, and on and on.

It is never a good idea to start your own business just to show people you can. If you do, people will see, but you are the one who will be left with what you started, whether it makes you happy or not, whether your heart is in it or not. However, if your heart is in it but there are those around you who tell you it can't be done, or at least not by you, that very well may be the impetus you need to DO it! If it's in you to do it, and you can't see, feel, or find any reason not to be able to do it, never let the odds keep you from pursuing what you know in your heart you were meant to do.

Dreams do not last forever; they tend to shrivel and die if left un-nurtured, unattended, uncared-for. Dreams, like flowers, are delicate and fragile things. Dreams can fade from unkind words or the slamming of a door in their face, unless they're supported and protected; unless, like flowers, they're watered, fertilized, put in the sunlight, and strengthened by belief, dedication, and perseverance.

If you—the reader of these words—have a dream buried deep within your being, or pressing against the window of your heart or soul, let it out! Bring it forth! Plant it in fertile soil, expose it to the sun, let it become the living, growing foundation upon which you build your true-life vocation. The success you so rightfully deserve as the Empress of your own Enterprise is not so very far away.

> *Somebody said that it couldn't be done,*
> *But he with a chuckle replied*
> *That "maybe it couldn't," but he would be one*
> *Who wouldn't say so till he'd tried.*
> *So he buckled right in with the trace of a grin*
> *On his face. If he worried he hid it.*
> *He started to sing as he tackled the thing.*
> *That couldn't be done, and he did it.*
>
> -Edgar A. Guest
> <u>It Couldn't Be Done</u>

Building the Foundation for Your Dream

Your dream is your foundation; it is what you build upon. It will support all the other floors as you build your business and create your masterpiece. Remember, it's YOUR dream, so be prepared to climb your own ladders, carry your own weight, and open your own doors. And, as you reap the rewards of your own success, remember the people who were there along the way—to encourage, support, and help you to your goal—and treat them as the very important people they are. For we may have the world's biggest or "best" dream, and we may work long and hard to achieve it, yet, in the truest form of reality, no one goes it alone without the help of someone! There are always people who will intervene on your behalf, make a phone call for you, or arrange an appointment or an introduction for you. What may seem trite to them in terms of effort could mean the equivalent of climbing Mt. Kilimanjaro to you. It is human nature to help. Don't forget it later, when you have it made! "Remember where you came from" is an old cliché I have used all my life.

Looking Back to Look Ahead

I once read an article that highlighted a successful businessperson's address to a high school graduating class, which offered the following insights:

> *When a successful businessperson speaks, pay attention; you might learn something helpful. A president of a large corporation was addressing a high school graduating class and wanted to give them the benefit of his knowledge. He knew he'd have to get their attention first. "If I could have hope for you as you go out into the world," he said, "I hope you fail. I hope you fail at something that is important to you, for failure, like nothing else, is able to stimulate the right kind of person to that extra action that always makes all the difference."*
>
> *This businessman had been through his own failures of one thing after another, and then read a story about Thomas Edison telling a group of high school students that he had tried 600 times and failed before he perfected the incandescent bulb. When*

asked if he was discouraged at so much failure, Mr. Edison is said to have replied that he didn't fail, he merely found 600 ways that did not work and learned at least one lesson from every one of them!

The businessman decided right then and there to follow Edison's example and learn one thing from every "lesson." He wrote his lessons down, put them into practice, and became a success—thanks to his many "ways that didn't work," and the lessons he learned from them.

And that can be us; every one of us who tried—and failed—and tried again. As long as we end on a note of trying again, we are not "doomed" to failure; we are destined for success with wisdom as our guide.

Forging the "Failure" Out of the Foundation

A good beginning makes a good ending.
-English Proverb

Things are always at their best in the beginning.
-Pascal, *Lettres provinciales*

The beginning is the most important part of the work.
-Plato, *The Republic*

It's easy to feel like a failure before you even start, if all you hear are the admonitions from those around you who offer their free advice: "You'll never make it work, so save yourself the trouble"; "You know you'll lose everything if you try to start your own business, so why bother?"; "You'd be better off with a real job"; "You've never succeeded at anything before, what makes you think you can do it now?"; "You've got nothing going for you—no capital, no credit, no credentials; all you have are pipe dreams"; "How do you expect to make it against all that competition out there?" And on and on and on, ad infinitum, and "for your own good," of course. Let us start to counter that negativity right here and now with some positive insights for you to ponder, today and any day the negativity starts to creep in. I always like to look at Grandma Barbee's Mini Book o' Quotes. Never let the negative creep in and deter you from your goal, your dream.

GRANDMA BARBEE'S
MINI BOOK OF QUOTES

Do not let what you cannot do interfere with what you can do.
   -John Wooden, college basketball coach

First say to yourself what you would be; and then do what you have to do.
                    -Epictetus, *Discourses*

Only those who dare to fail greatly can ever achieve greatly.
                         -Anonymous

A great pleasure in life is doing what people say you cannot do.
                    -Walter Gagehot

Our chief want in life is somebody who will make us do what we can.
                    -Ralph Waldo Emerson

Unless you try to do something beyond what you have already mastered, you will never grow.
                    -Ronald E. Osborn

We judge ourselves by what we feel capable of doing, while others judge us by what we have already done.
                    -Henry Wadsworth Longfellow

All great accomplishments have a simple beginning.

-Anonymous

There's only one success: to be able to spend your life in your own way.

-Christopher Morley

There can be no happiness if the things we believe in are different from the things we do.

-Freya Stark

If you've made up your mind you can do something, you're absolutely right. Whether you think you can or you can't, you're right.

-Henry Ford

Failure is not the worst thing in the world. The very worst is not to try. The only time you can't afford to fail is the last time you try.

-Charles Kettering

They can do all because they think they can.

-Virgil, *Aeneid*

To be a champ you have to believe in yourself when nobody else will.

-Sugar Ray Robinson

Hitch your wagon to a star.
-Ralph Waldo Emerson, *Civilization*

Things to Ponder Before Getting Committed:

Take calculated risks. That is quite different from being rash.
-General George Patton
(from a letter to his son)

Something to consider when starting your business: How is your track record of sticking to New Year's resolutions? In following through with things you intended to do? In sticking with a new interest for more than a month or so? If everything you ever intended to do got lost in the shuffle early in the game, or if you tend to lose interest in a new project after a short time, perhaps this plan to go into business will follow suit.

Why not consider "sampling" the business before actually jumping in? Examples: If going into the cookie-making business, offer to bake cookies for a local fund-raiser for a week or two. If setting up a bridal shop is your dream, offer to make the gowns and accessories for someone you know, at cost and on schedule. If it's mail order you've a mind to master, try placing some small ads to sell just one or two items you have, for a month or so. Want to open a restaurant? Volunteer to help out at a family shelter, cooking, serving, and observing the preparation and presentation process. You get the picture.

Even if you're 100 percent sure it's what you want to do right now, give yourself the necessary reinforcement by having a trial period. Try on the activity, the dream, before your hopes and funds are invested. That trial period may have some additional benefits, such as learning more about what it takes to succeed.

What of the Risk?

Not risking is an easy way of losing what you didn't even know you could have! Starting a business is a risk. We cannot live without taking risks. We cannot grow without some risk. We cannot ever know what could have been without taking risks. If you believe in yourself, you will want to risk whatever it takes. HOWEVER, there are "rules" to follow before you go for it.

Rules for Risking

1. **ASSESS** what you have to gain and all that you could lose. Consider the worst thing that could happen if you go for it, and decide if you could live with that. Write down all the pros and cons. Remember that what makes it a risk is the element of the unknown—which cannot be accounted for.

2. **ACT** on it once you have decided to do so. Decisions are not actions. Although there is such a thing as "the perfect time," most of us are never prepared for it because we're so preoccupied with all the things we have to do FIRST. Be prepared for your opportunity—it'll probably show

up when you least expect it—and be ready to act on it, to take that first step.

3. **TRUST** that something will happen. Taking a risk is like jumping from an airplane in flight. Between the jump and the landing there is nothing you can do but hope and pray that the parachute will open, you'll land on friendly turf, and you won't be hurt. If you did your part beforehand, the chute will open, you'll land where you were supposed to land, unhurt, and your ride back to town will even be conveniently waiting for you nearby. However, no one can know for sure whether or not a big wind will come by, blowing you off course, out of your projected landing area; or if the chute will get caught on something, hanging you up for awhile; or if a wild (or even domestic) animal might be in the area, lending its own new twist to your situation; or if the car intended to take you to town will have a flat or an accident—quirks and quips of Mother Nature and Father Fate.

4. **ACCEPT** your success when it comes. Accept compliments, praise, and profits. Feel pride in your work. Yet no matter how big the payoff, maintain your perspective. You're not God, and you can't guarantee your success will last forever. Success, you may have heard, is not permanent. But then, neither is failure.

There are plenty of things you will need and questions you need to ask once you have decided to go ahead and build your business. Ask yourself a few more good questions to help build the right foundation for your success. The more you understand your business and your motivation, the better off you will be.

- Even if it's a great idea, am I the one to do it?
- Am I thinking business? Money? Self-satisfaction? Or a good mixture of all three?
- Is it worth my time, effort, energy, and passion?
- Knowing myself as I do, does it seem likely that I'll give this my all and still want to be doing it next year at this time?

The lights are all green. There is no need to wait. Start proceeding down the path to materialize your dream, because a great idea turns out to be somebody else's "brainchild" if you put off doing something about it when it's yours. If you want the credit and the success that goes with it, pursue it with all your heart, now. You cannot discover new oceans unless you have the courage to lose sight of the shore!

Starting Time

You can start a business any time. You don't have to wait until the new year, the beginning of a month, or the beginning of a week. When you feel ready, when the desire stirs you, move on it at that moment, even if it's the middle of winter, the middle of the month, or the middle of the night. That feeling to get started is called inspiration. Get up and put it to good use.

Start writing. Write down everything that's important to you, and why, and how you plan to achieve it. Give yourself plenty of space to add on later as you think of more to say. This will be a list of what you want from life. Keep this in your "Building My Dream" file. Feed it daily.

CHAPTER TWO

GOALS AND THE BUSINESS STRUCTURE

Ready...Set Goals!

When athletes run in a race, they have one thought, one central focus before them and paramount in their mind—the finish line! With this illustration in mind, picture your goals. Determine the purpose for your business—give yourself a sense of direction. It gives you a focus, a goal to aim for.

Without a sense of direction it is easy to stray off course and amble about aimlessly. Use your personal, rational judgment when making goals. Make them obtainable. If you make them so extraordinary that it would take a miracle to reach them, rethink them. Instead of striving for a once-in-a-lifetime lottery win, realize the true value of receiving daily blessings. To miss reaching your goals would only serve to frustrate you and cause you to give up. First, set short, obtainable goals and work up to the far stretched goals. This will give you the fulfilling satisfaction of attainment, ultimately followed by the quest of more challenging goals.

Eight Quick Success Tips for Reaching Your Goal

1. Extend your mental desires to the physical form: write them out. Be specific. For instance: "I want to have my business

plan completed by January 1." "I want to have my financing in place by March 30." "I want to begin production by May 1."

2. Give your goals that in-depth dimension: picture yourself achieving what you want, and be generous with details. Make it a part of your day to affirm what you want—morning, noon, and night.

3. Say them out loud—and often.

4. Surround yourself with positive energy: upbeat, supportive friends; encouraging books; motivational tapes; inspiring words of wisdom.

5. Prepare, train, and strive with an unrelenting mindset for the goal. Believe in yourself: you're worth the effort.

6. Believe in your dreams: they are your inspiration.

On Being Aware—An Affirmation

What I want will remain a preference. If I start to feel addicted and act addicted to my goals, whether those goals are wealth, prestige, fame, or even helping others, I will step back and reevaluate where I am going and why. No "goal" will control me! And no goal will make me abuse my family, friends, employees, or any others for my own selfish ends. My preferences will guide me and keep me moving forward in a positive way. Let these affirmations be your personal guide; evaluate them, post them, keep them, and be sure you really understand them.

Some "Ready-Made" Resolutions

Almost everyone needs some help in focusing from time to time. Make a resolution, write it down, and review it from time to time. The following are "ready-made" ones which you might find useful, or help you come up with your own to live by:

- I will achieve my goal.
- I will organize my thoughts into a plan.
- I will develop and maintain a positive attitude toward success.
- I will let my thoughts take me wherever they will—I will be creative!
- I will let everyone be my teacher—I will discount no one.
- I will work smarter, not harder, while remembering that it can be hard work to get to doing things the smart way.
- I will not be afraid to take risks— since big payoffs require big risks— but I will use common sense and care before taking any risk.
- I know procrastination gets me nowhere. I will make decisions, and then act on them. I can always procrastinate tomorrow!
- I will keep on keeping on.

- I will associate with others who are like-minded and upbeat.
- I will expect good things and be enthusiastic about my expectations.
- I will be ready for new opportunities by being prepared. Knowledge leads to preparation.
- I won't do anything I'll be ashamed of. I will maintain my high morals.
- I will ignore uninformed opinions. Ignorance contributes nothing but harm or negativity.
- I will be happy for each small achievement on my way to the big one, and will reward myself in some way for each one.
- I will not perpetuate errors or mistakes. As soon as I spot one, I'll fix it.
- I will not be a slave to rules and regulations that don't work. Just because people say "It's always been done that way" is no reason for me to do it that way without question.

RESOLVE is: determination, loyalty, courage, devotedness, persistence, backbone, strength of will, a show of character, an optimistic mindset that is focused. It is an attitude that says: "Regardless of circumstances, obstacles, or what may come my way, I am going to run the race before me. I am going to finish this race; I am going to win it and receive the reward!" Don't fret if you have to make an occasional adjustment in you attitude.

It's normal. Then once again, stand firm and resolve to do all that is necessary for your goals to reach fruition.

Best Rules

There are rules for everything, and therefore there are rules to planning out your business. The following are my rules to get you going:

- **Write it down**
  - Your goals
  - Places to go
  - People to meet
  - Things to do
  - Answers to give
  - Books to read
- **Be specific**
  - By March 29, I will have brought in $100,000 in new sales.
  - By midnight tonight, I'll have finished reading the three business proposals.
  - I will bake chocolate chip cookies after work today for our business meeting tomorrow.
- **Have a Plan B**
  - I will buy a frozen chocolate chip cheesecake to keep in my freezer in the event that I don't have time to make the chocolate chip cookies for the business meeting.
- **Have a business slogan to live by**
  - We're here because of you.
  - At Fairytale Bakery, we believe in Beauty and the Yeast.

- No job is too small for us if it's big enough to bother you.
- At Empress Beauty Spa, we give you the Royal Treatment.

Giving Goals Flexibility to Work for You and Your Business Life

Flexibility is paramount to keeping your sanity in all of the madness that will ensue as your business begins to take shape. There are several "tricks" that I have learned and seen practiced by others which will help to give you some flexibility.

- Allow yourself twice as much time as you think something will take. If you don't need the extra time, use it for another project on your "to do" list, or reward yourself by doing something you enjoy (read a magazine or book that you've been wanting to start, write a letter, go for a walk, get a pedicure). That extra time will reduce stress and pressure.

- Set realistic goals and be open to changes in your plans. You may prefer to work on your books or get the inventory done as scheduled, but a business acquaintance or friend calls, is going to be in town for just a few hours, and wants to see you. This is not an interruption of your plans. It's called "Life." And Life is what happens while you're busy doing other things. Don't lose your life in the process of business, enhance it.

- Change big projects into smaller, easier-to-complete tasks. By breaking things up into smaller tasks, progress can be readily seen. You may not have time to take on the whole project today, but you can finish a portion of it.

- Reward yourself for accomplishments immediately. Take that half hour coffee break after a grueling work session. Go to a favorite restaurant for lunch after landing a new client. Soak in a bubble bath after a great day at work!

- Realize that you are not perfect (nor is anyone else), so any mistakes you make are just part of the process of learning, growing, and striving for perfection. Don't let fear of not being perfect keep you from doing what you need to do.

- Try doing all those things you enjoy doing (but have been putting off) first, since they usually get put to the bottom of the list in favor of the things you're supposed to do first.

- Get those things you enjoy least done as soon as possible in the day—then get on with enjoying the day.

- Lack of progress tends to prevent us from making any progress. Keep a diary of your progress and read it often. It will serve as a basis for future planning and refining; more importantly, it will spur you on to additional accomplishments.

- Stay focused. Remove yourself from distractions, or remove the distractions (such as food, TV, magazines, company, phone calls, etc.). Be honest enough to recognize your distractions.

- Keep a long list of "things to do" with you at all times so you are never in a "what do I need to do?" mode.

Organizing the Business Structure

"The business of America is business!"

—Calvin Coolidge

As your dream begins to take on a form, one of the first essential steps in giving shape to that form is to decide which legal structure best suits your business and personal needs.

We will assume that by now you have discussed your personal preferences, options, and financial position with your accountant, and even your lawyer, and have set aside your predetermined thoughts or opinions. You have studied the subject in depth, spending many hours at the library, attending various business-related and SBA seminars, to discover all the facts for yourself before zeroing in on the exact structure of your new company. All of this study and conferencing have no doubt reinforced your own analytical conclusions.

It is very important that all paperwork be properly and legally filed with the proper agencies so that you do not encounter any problems, such as improper filing with city, state, or federal agencies. You will need to select one of the following structures for your business:

Business Types	Pros	Cons
Sole Proprietorship Owner has full control of business.	• Easiest • Least Expensive • No Corporate Taxes • One Tax Return (Owner's)	• Unlimited Personal Liability of Owner • High Risk to Raise Capital
Partnership Two or more people own and control the business.	• Easier • Lower Cost • No Corporate Taxes • Simple Tax Return (Owners') • Easier to Raise Capital	• Unlimited Personal Liability of Owners

Limited Partnership Consists of General partners and Limited partners. General partners run the business and Limited partners contribute specified sums of money.	• Limited Partners Are Limited in Their Liability • Easier to Raise Capital	• Requires Written Legal Document Signed By All Partners • More Complicated
Corporation Company created as a separate entity from any of the owners or stockholders.	• Separates Business and Personal Assets • Liability of Founders Is Limited • Easier to Raise Capital • No Tax On Capital Invested Through Stock Purchases	• Added Expense of Filing Two Tax Returns • Much More Complicated • Requires Formalized and Documented Procedures

Sole Proprietorship

This type of business is easy to start, you make all the decisions, and you get all the profits. It is less expensive to start than a corporation and there are no corporate taxes to pay; the owner files one tax return. The owner is permitted to deduct any losses that might have been incurred during the beginning start up of a business from other sources of personal income.

One of the main disadvantages to this form of structure is <u>unlimited personal liability</u>. As the sole proprietor, you become personally responsible and liable for the debts, judgments, or the financial losses that could occur due to failure or other disasters. As a sole proprietor, you might find it difficult to raise capital. If the owner dies or becomes incapacitated, the business often comes to a standstill. As with many things, it has a higher risk and therefore a higher payoff.

On the bright side, the owner makes all of the decisions and reaps all of the rewards for the success of the business. As a sole proprietor, you decide whether to spend more on advertising, less on salaries, buy a new sign, or remodel. The money you spend or choose to invest comes out your pocket.

Partnership

Two or more people own this type of a business and it is very similar to the sole proprietorship shared between multiple parties. Again, it is less expensive to start than a corporation, just like a sole proprietorship. If you enter into a partnership, it is imperative that you draw up a written agreement between you and your partner(s) to prevent possible misunderstandings in the future. The agreement should make the relationship clear, defining who makes what decisions and how the business will be run. Partnerships usually enjoy more access to capital for two reasons; each partner can contribute his or her share, and loans to partnerships are usually easier to obtain and are for larger dollar amounts.

The disadvantages to a partnership include that each partner is legally responsible for the debts of the other partners. Partners must divide the profits equally, even though one partner may believe he or she contributed more than the other. The final concern is that disagreements between partners on how best to run the company can tear apart the best of friendships. Enter into business with friends carefully and with your eyes wide open.

Limited Partnership

This form of business consists of general partners and limited partners. The general partners are responsible for managing the company; the limited partners contribute a specified sum of money only. Forming a limited partnership requires a written legal document that is signed by all partners. There are several items that must be included in this document; contact an attorney specializing in business corporations and partnership law.

In a limited partnership, each partner is only liable to the amount they have invested into the business. As a result, limited partners receive a specified percentage of any profits.

The general partners are responsible for the daily operations of the business. They make the decisions as specified in the legal arrangement. In some cases, the general partners provide more of the sweat and therefore receive a larger percentage of the profits. This profit percentage may be negotiated depending on the work required, capital invested, and other factors.

The limited partners are really just investors. They provide capital to the business and in return receive a percentage of the profits of the business. The success or failure of the business cannot really be affected by the limited partners. They are "along for the ride."

Corporation

The corporation is a recognized legal entity that stands separate from any individual. In other words, you separate the business interests from your personal assets and create a new legal entity that is bestowed with its own rights, responsibilities, and functions.

The personal liability of the founders is limited to the amount of money put into the corporation, excluding unpaid taxes, of course. A corporation does not pay tax on capital it receives in exchange for its stock because it is invested capital, not earned income. When the business owner wishes to raise money, a corporation is more desirable to attract investors for the purpose of raising capital. The corporation's capital can be increased by issuing and selling additional shares of stock throughout its existence.

The disadvantages of incorporating include the added expense of filing two tax returns, one individual and one corporate. If financing is obtained by a corporation from sources such as a bank, the lending source may require a personal guarantee by the owner(s), thereby eliminating the limited liability advantage of a corporation to the terms of the loan agreement. The corporate minutes require additional time to maintain and keep current.

A corporation may exist only with the permission of state government. "Articles of Incorporation" must be filed with the secretary of your state, and this document will usually require that names and addresses of at least three "Incorporators" be listed, as well as the name and address of the corporation and its purpose, the number and type of shares of stock that are to be issued, and the amount of capital the corporation has to operate with.

Upon approving the submitted document, the secretary of state will issue a "Certificate of Incorporation" or "Charter," at which time the word "Incorporated" or "Corporation," or the abbreviation, will need to be added to the company name. Once these steps are completed and the corporation is chartered, the necessary city and state licenses and permits will be required before any further business activity is conducted. The State Corporation Commission (SCC) will need to issue your SCC identification number.

Incorporating your business enables you to raise extra needed capital by selling company stock shares. In exchange for money, people buy shares of stock in your corporation, which represent partial ownership and entitlement to a percentage of the corporation's profits. There are several forms of corporations: Nonprofit Corporations, S Corporations, and C Corporations.

Consult your certified public accountant (CPA) and/ or lawyer to review your company's status and give her advice for the corporation type that fits your needs.

3. City, State, and Federal Requirements

LAW: The custom of the kingdom
-Justice North

City Requirements

We have now come to the point of taking our first steps into the reality of the business world. If you operate in a city or township, there are city licenses and permits to obtain in order to operate your business. Depending on the type of business you are applying for, certain regulations exist. For example, restaurants, beauty shops, barber shops, spas, dry cleaners, day-care centers, nursing centers, etc., must pass health department inspection standards to obtain licensing. Other businesses such as exterminators, plumbers, electricians, contractors, painters, etc., must meet bonding and licensing requirements and are subject to city and state inspections. Doctors, dentists, lawyers, certified public accountants, cosmetologists, pharmacists, veterinarians, etc., must pass state-certified board examinations and obtain city licenses before opening up their professions.

Each city and state varies in policies and requirements. If you are in any way unclear as to what regulations apply to your business, you should call your city hall offices in your telephone book for local listings or call information. Ask for the city clerk or the administrative offices. Other sources of information include the Better Business Bureau, the state regulation office, and the state licensing department.

State Requirements

State government has broad powers to regulate business. You will need to call or personally go to your state capital. Not all states are the same, but usually you will need to apply for an Employers Identification Number and state tax number. Labor-related information may also be needed if you plan on hiring employees. Some states require employees to have a sheriff's card, a health card, etc., depending on the type of work they will be doing. <u>It is your responsibility to know the requirements</u>. Among other requirements for employees are: workers compensation insurance, wage and hour information, I-9 and W-2 forms, unemployment withholding taxes, etc. Be sure to ask for any and all information regarding employees if you are unfamiliar with labor laws.

If you still need additional information, look online in your state government's Website for information and e-mail your questions. Look for the listing in the state section of your local phone book for the state public information officer. Call the number, ask for an information packet, or for the location of the nearest office where you can get the information you need.

Federal Requirements

Yes, you are just beginning to deal with "paperwork." You must also obtain the necessary federal forms and numbers. Visit the IRS.gov Website for information that will familiarize you with additional forms and information you need. Most of the federal requirements center around taxes. You can obtain File Form SS-4 from your state capital, which is the paperwork required to file for a <u>Federal Identification Number.</u> It usually takes about four weeks to receive this number, which is your identifier to the federal government for taxes on the business and its employees.

As the business owner, you are required to pay <u>Federal Unemployment Taxes (FUTA)</u> on your employees. You are required by law to file those FUTA taxes quarterly on all existing employees.

The <u>Federal Income Taxes (FICA)</u> are the bimonthly or monthly federal taxes that are withheld from employee paychecks as is the law of the federal government. These taxes are then matched by the same percentage by the employer. These FICA taxes are known as "employee matching taxes" and are usually paid with a "deposit slip" (sent to you by the IRS in a booklet) to an authorized bank. The paperwork explaining these taxes may be obtained from a local address in your city. Again, look in the local phone book under the "United States Government" section for "Federal Employment Information Offices." If all else fails, call the Federal Information Center's toll-free number (800-359-3997). If the line is too darn busy, go to the official Web portal of the federal government, FirstGov.gov.

An employee is required to fill out an <u>I-9 Form</u> at the time of employment. This form documents your employee's eligibility to work. These forms may be obtained at the local Internal Revenue Service (IRS) office or your CPA's office.

NOTE: If you are in any way still in the dark after searching through the Websites and doing your own research concerning the requirements and paperwork that you are obligated to file and keep records of, do not hesitate to call the IRS office in Austin, Texas, at 800-TAX-1040. Also request Publication Number 334, "Tax Guide for Small Business." Published annually, it is a mini how-to book, which explains what forms must be filed and why, what deductions you are entitled to, and different tax laws and bookkeeping systems from sole proprietorships to corporations. The publication also includes sample tax forms, plus information pertinent to filing your tax returns.

All of this will no doubt help you, but major assistance will come from YOUR accountant. Find one you can work with well and can have confidence in.

Not that you might need this particular information until you retire or sell the assets of your company, but because I want this book to be thorough, I have included this bit of information.

Dissolving A Corporation

Somewhere along the way, you might need to dissolve your corporation, whether it is because you want to retire, sell the assets of your corporation, or you find your dream isn't working out. You will need to contact your State Corporation Commission's Corporation Department (listed in the "State Government" section of the phone book, under Corporation Commission) and ask for the "Requirements for Dissolution." This document gives instructions for dissolving your corporation and several documents you must file. You will be asked to specify whether your corporation is a Profit or Nonprofit organization. A Nonprofit business isn't the focus of this book.

Dissolving a Profit Corporation:

- The first document you must file is the "Statement of Intent to Dissolve." An endorsement with the acknowledgment that it has been filed will be mailed back to you.
- At this point, if you have not already started, begin to terminate the corporation's business affairs.

- The following state agencies must then be contacted, and you must request a clearance of dissolution from each agency: State Taxation and Revenue Department, Audit and Compliance Section State Department of Labor, Employment Division State Corporation Commission, and Corporation Department

Clearances from the above agencies require that there be no outstanding taxes, contributions, interest, or penalties due. Each agency will research your corporation Courtroom dramas do not touch most of our lives. The law of government, on the other hand, controls almost every activity of common interest—fixing the pothole in front of the house, running public schools, regulating day-care centers, supervising the workplace, cleaning up the environment, and deciding whether anyone gets a building permit.

- in regards to what, if anything, is owed them. If your corporation's account is current, a "Clearance for Dissolution" is granted and will be mailed to you. If not, each agency will inform you what is due and hold Clearance for Dissolution until the fees are paid. You must have written clearance from each agency in order to proceed.

- After clearances have been granted by each agency, you must then file the Articles of Dissolution, along with the three clearances, to the State Corporation Commission, Corporation Department.

NOTE: Filing fees are required for the Statement of Intent to Dissolve and the Articles of Dissolution documents; the amounts are specified in the instructions.

Dissolving a Sole Proprietor/Partnership:

- The business owner has to make sure all liens, taxes, bankruptcies, or other encumbrances are satisfied.
- End of year taxes and any other accounting business must be taken care of through the usual procedures with the accountant.

Other Government Help for Official Business

The government is officially online at FirstGov.gov. The government services and information available are inconceivable! Check it out in depth and then go to additional sites suggested, such as the Small Business Administration (SBA.gov). These are independent federal agencies created by Congress to specifically help small businesses grow and prosper. For government information by phone call 800-FED-INFO (800-333-1636). The government's official online library consists of more than a hundred publications on all business topics and they are freely yours for the asking.

For a free copy of the SBA's "Directory of Business Development" publications, go by and pick it up at your local office, or write and request a copy from: SBA Publications, P.O. Box 15434, Fort Worth, Texas 76119. You may also contact the SBA through the Small Business Answer Desk at 800-9-ASK-SBA, between the hours of 8:30 a.m. to 5:00 p.m. (Eastern time). The Answer Desk is a service provided by the SBA's Office of Business Initiatives, Education and Training. The Answer Desk can give you answers and/or guidance to your business needs with information and a referral system. The SBA can also serve as a potential avenue for funding through SBA-secured loans.

Several publications are available which explain the "ropes" of financing a business, cash management, and borrowing. There are numerous publications on venture capital, banking, business plans—you name it, they've got it!

CHAPTER THREE

THE COMMINGLED BUSINESSWOMAN

Barbee's Ode to Businesswomen

Gifted entrepreneurial women don't just spring from a sudden inspiration, nor do they attain greatness through luck overnight. Every milestone achieved came from a thousand steps of preparation. Every moment of public gain reflects hours of personal sacrifice. Every smile in public represents a personal tear in private. Business experts call it "paying dues." If it truly were to have a title, it would be "The Art of Perseverance." And, it would turn our efforts into noteworthiness, our hopes into achievements, and our dreams into priceless realities.

Business Connections

As a woman, jumping into business could be referred to as an adventure, a preoccupation, an obsession. Divided feelings exist about power, authenticity, female ambition, and gender roles. Don't be deceived or intimidated; it's a wonderful venture and experience—albeit one filled with potential dangers and pitfalls, complex ambivalences, not-so-simple truths, and personal discipline. Although you can leave your success to serendipity (good luck!), · you should think about stacking the cards in your favor with a little preplanning and forethought before jumping in with both feet to make the landing safer.

My goal for this book is to make the learning part as simple and fun as possible while also encouraging you to discover new insights and approaches, and to develop sound judgment skills. Knowledge is a powerful tool that will serve you well in the world of business.

The Human Connection

Flour and sugar may both come in five-pound bags and cost exactly the same amount. They may sit side by side on grocery shelves, being freely available in matching quantities to the very same shoppers, with each being as indispensable as the other for its particular properties. Yet no one would—for even one second—suggest that they are so alike, so "equal," that it doesn't matter which bag one buys. We all know that flour and sugar are not fungible! Nor would we want them to be.

It's time—after centuries of perhaps being thought of as less than males, and decades of perhaps wanting to be exactly like males—for females to acknowledge, and revel in, their differences from men. Men may even take advantage of us because of some of our differences, but that just highlights—again—the very differences that come into play between us. As humans, we all share in the Homo sapiens experience. As men and women, separately, some of us can and do have babies; and some of us do have semi-dependable mood swings or "personality challenges" every so often. It's kind of built into the system and may innocently overlap into the workplace in one way or another.

Finally, regarding the man-woman thing, we should be looking more at the commonalties that we share—our human ties—rather than the differences that separate us which require special laws, amendments, policies, and regulations. If "others" think so, maybe that's why we see things as "a man's world." After all these years, maybe Nature is trying to tell us something.

> *If you are not afraid to face the music, you may someday lead the band.*
> -Johnathan Swift

What You Need To Know

Putting yourself "out there" in the world of business requires you to shake off your complacency and brush up on your co-ed cognizance. We all know that men are individuals and want to be "judged" on their own merit, as opposed to being lumped together in some "all men are alike" category. The same is true that all women are not alike; while they're all still women, we need to remind ourselves of these two nuances.

There seems to exist this weird belief among males that it's really quite funny to "shock" females with their "locker-room" jokes and stories. Women who then are shocked—or, more aptly put, disgusted—are considered prudes, challenges, sticks-in-the-mud, party-poopers, or whatever the term of the day happens to be. Although just about all women understand the nature of sexual thoughts and desires in men, the opposite cannot be said, in most cases. It is true that many women play up to that male nature by flaunting the very things that keep the male nature so tuned. It is not at all surprising that males respond to this ploy. However, what may come as a surprise to such men is that not all women who have blonde hair and wear short skirts or red lipstick are saying, "Please tell me all the dirty jokes you know, make crude remarks about particular parts of my body, and then invite me to go to bed with you." Surprisingly enough, although some men may interpret it that way, many women are just saying, "Look at me—I feel good about myself and I hope that everyone who sees me will feel confident that I can do my job!"

If one man is somehow offended or distracted by a particular woman's appearance (in a place where it may impact on him, such as the office, at a business meeting, or in any official business context), it is quite possible that other men (and even other women) might be offended or distracted as well. It is in that case where the woman is "out to lunch" on what is and is not appropriate for the business world.

Now that you're the woman in charge, it will be up to you to address this issue. It should be no different than addressing the issue of a male wearing muscle shirts or tight pants to the office. It is only a matter of appropriateness, NOT sexism, since most office attire policies strive to avoid whatever would engender more controversy over one's sex.

Here are a few sexually-slanted generalities worth noting as you decide on your personal attire and dress policies for the office.

- Men are easily distracted by sexy-looking women. It is "normal" for men to notice, stare at, think about, and make excuses to deal with sexy-looking women. This does not mean that it is "okay," should be encouraged or condoned, or even ignored. It is to be dealt with. Use "business" common sense.

- Women cannot change men's nature, any more than men can change women's nature. However, it is in our best interests to understand each other's nature and act accordingly when business in involved.

- One's personal life is one thing; one's business life is another.

- You cannot control or change your basic nature, but you can and must control your business behavior and your business dress.

- You are showing your ignorance as well as your "assets" if you wear miniskirts, tight sweaters, low-cut dresses, or the like, and expect men not to stare or respond like typical males. It will be difficult to be taken seriously in the business world by men OR women if you choose to dress other than professionally. If you really do not know how to dress for business, then ask for help from other businesswomen.

- You are displaying even more ignorance if you try to justify

wearing such outfits and then still get
annoyed at the men who comment,
stare, or make unwanted advances.

You can control a lot of the interactions with men. This includes your behavior, meeting venues, and conversation topics. As a businesswoman, and when you have employees, you have to establish the control that you and your staff need to have between each other, customers, and business associates.

Handshakes are more businesslike than hugs and don't compromise your position as a businesswoman. As a businesswoman, you will be shaking a lot of hands, so learn to have a good firm one.

Try to use gender-neutral comments because they work better than gender-slanted ones. Example: "I like the way you handled the Bennett account," instead of "I like your dress" or "I like your tie." Under ordinary conditions, they would be just ordinary comments, but under conditions wherein an employee wishes to make a case for sexual harassment, such comments could accumulate into something else. Would you want it on the front page of your local newspaper? Politicians are always being quoted—or misquoted. If you're making a name for yourself, some reporter might want to make a name for him or herself by revealing a side of you not meant for public consumption.

Be very aware of what you say in public. Note: it should not even be in your heart to use language that might come back to haunt you (ethnic slurs, racial put-downs, sexual innuendoes, etc.). You don't want something to even sound like something you would have said.

Stop what you don't like, want, or appreciate as soon as you experience it. "No, I do not like blonde jokes." "Please do not sit on my desk." And don't settle for the old "excuse my French" line when a person uses vulgar language and then realizes you are there. It is not French, and it is not acceptable. And you may tell him in ANY language.

Change is inevitable, and sometimes is extremely difficult for certain people to accept. If it is seen as normal, natural, and good for all concerned, it will eventually smooth itself out, or the "unyielding" will drift away.

> *It ain't what you say, it's the way that you say it.*
> -John Cushman
>
> *A man that's got something to say don't need all week to make his point.*
> -Joe Louis

Understanding the Language

No matter how savvy we think we are, we may occasionally slip and "misuse" (or be shocked or disturbed at someone else's "misuse" of) our mother tongue. We must remember that long before there was such a thing as being "politically correct," there was an English language with perfectly good words capable of conveying just about everything we needed to convey. As we became more sophisticated in particular areas of life (like computers, for example), we added words to specialized lexicons to reflect that additional dimension.

However our language may have expanded, we have not eliminated the meanings of words we've all come to know and love since birth (or shortly thereafter), even though we've come to be more sensitive to the various nuances of those meanings. In our quest to be taken seriously as women in the world of business, let us not go overboard by demanding a change in anyone's vocabulary when we hear perfectly good and basically gender-neutral words (such as chairman, foreman, spokesman), no matter how much we may cringe at hearing those words (consider the word human). The meaning of the word "man" has not changed. It still means an adult male person, and it also still means a member of the species Homo sapiens or all the members of the species collectively, without regard to sex in all good conscience. Let's save our energy for more important things and educate those who are unaware as we go through time.

To take this advice a step further, it is very important to understand that the world of business, in and of itself, has its own language. Although some words and terms may be familiar, some may just sound familiar, only to prove to our embarrassment to be something else entirely. Whether we've heard them all or not, understand them or not, many will be bandied about with abandon in the corporate commonwealth, so it behooves us to be conversant with the lingo. I would like to suggest that you also make a list of new words or terms you hear from time to time. People respect and admire you when you speak their language, and appreciate it when you do not interrupt every sentence with, "I'm sorry, what does that stand for?" or "What does that mean?" Or, worse yet, assume a meaning that changes the whole nature of the conversation or the business at hand.

In addition to the language of a business, you'll find there are many other affiliated "languages" you'll probably pick up as you go along, and each one contains a string of words and phrases you've either never heard before, or will soon wish you didn't have to hear. There's legalese, economese, Wall Streetese, newspaperese, officialese, federalese, computerese; and within each language, any number of dialects, known as "shoptalk." You may or may not want to learn them all, but you will be exposed to many of them. Keeping a notebook of such new words and terms is a good idea, or you can jot them down in this book!

Communication Confusion Clarified

There are some simple suggestions that I am including to help you navigate the business waters and remain intact:

- Use the words you know, correctly and precisely.
- Bring new words into your vocabulary cautiously (using them incorrectly is worse than doing without). You might sound

uneducated or low class. Sometimes saying less is more.

- Reduce misunderstandings by speaking clearly, saying what you mean, and meaning what you say.
- Avoid confusion or lack of communication by giving clear instructions. Example: "See that it gets done" is not clear. Who shall do the "seeing," what exactly is "it," when is it to be done by, and what does "done" look like?
- Be sure that those on the receiving end interpret your message the way that you intend it. Example: "Be sure to charge the batteries" could end up getting you another item on your monthly credit card statement. Better to say, "Remember to put the batteries in the charger."
- Words are tools; use them correctly and to add interest to what you say. You cannot separate them from your ideas, so select the words that best set your ideas aflame.

> *I avoid looking forward or backward, and try to keep looking upward.*
> -Charlotte Bronte
>
> *People create their own questions because they're afraid to look straight. All you have to do is look straight and see the road, and when you see it, don't sit looking at it—walk.*
> -Ayn Rand

Staying on Top of It All

So, how do you stay on top of the game? You have to be able to keep a strong personal life and a productive business life. The section will give you some hints and pointers to help along the way. Feel free to remember these and add to them those items that you find work for you.

Five "Feel Good" Factors

You'll Feel Good If You:

1. Allow yourself to enjoy both your work and your play. How you "feel" during an activity greatly affects how

well you perform and how you're going to feel after the activity.

2. Allow yourself to indulge in those frivolous, fanciful fun-time activities that always make you feel good. Forget what others say about what you like to do.

3. Forget about living up to others' expectations, or conforming to the molds they've set out for you. You feel good when you "go with the flow" of your own nature, your own personality, whatever that shapes up to be.

4. Believe in your own needs, which includes doing nothing when that's what you feel you need to do. You can't feel good if you let others pressure you into doing something every minute of your waking day.

5. Do the things you do for the sake of doing them. If you want to do something, do it; if you love doing it, do it. If you feel the need to justify it, perhaps it's not really making you feel all that good.

We often do things that make us feel good. It is important that we also understand the basic reason that we do them. In business, make sure you are doing the "right" things for the "right" reasons.

Quick Quiz on Queenly Qualities

To succeed in business, it helps to understand the qualities we need to develop and display. Answer the following, and then check the box below for the answers.

1. Being able to reduce complex problems to their simplest terms takes...?
2. Making your own decisions, taking steps to accomplish your goals, and keeping yourself up-to-date on what you need to do are signs of...?
3. Your natural ability to comprehend, analyze, and follow through is reflected in your...?
4. When you educate yourself to improve your product or service, understand your competition, and pay attention to public perception of what you do, you're working at...?
5. As an organizer who cares about good work habits, you have...?
6. Taking charge comes easily when you know exactly what needs to be done. This takes...?
7. You may be daydreaming, but you're using your...?
8. You share information, believe in weekly meetings with your work team, and ask about the things that

matter to them, because one of the things that is important to you is…?

9. You realize that some people get ahead in life without seeming to do anything, and most people would say it's because of…?

10. You're careful, conscientious, and consistent. You've developed…?

ANSWERS

1. Common sense
2. Self-reliance
3. Overall intelligence
4. Knowing your field
5. The ability to get things done
6. Leadership
7. Creative imagination
8. Being a team player
9. A great inheritance
10. Good habits

He took my glasses off and he said, "Without your glasses, why, you're beautiful." I said, "without my glasses, you're not half bad either."

-Kit Hollerbach

Giving Yourself the Once-Over

Common Scents. If you're in the habit of wearing perfume or other scents, consider these points: a) what smells good to you may smell offensive to another; b) what seems "light" to you may come over as heady to others; c) some people are allergic to various perfumes and lotions; d) alcohol-based scents are altered by heat; what starts out as mild and inoffensive at home can end up intensified on the job as the alcohol evaporates; e) if there are four women in the workplace all wearing their own scents, common sense will tell you that a conflict of scents will occur.

Smiling. You can smile with your mouth, or you can smile with your face. If you don't know the difference, you can be sure others do. If you sincerely feel friendly, let your face know about it.

Mindless Behaviors. Do you twiddle with your hair, bite or pick at your fingernails, drum your fingers, click an ink pen off and on, or tap your toes? Those annoying little trespasses can creep into your personae.

Decisions. Whether it's a big deal or a little deal, what to have for lunch or which wine to have with which fish, somebody could be noticing that you have a hard time making decisions. Hmm…could that be translated into the business you?

Attitude. A little thing that makes a BIG difference. No matter how you look, speak, walk, or act, you cannot hide how you feel. A good, uplifting, happy, purposeful, and positive attitude will always find its way to the surface of the complete businesswoman. Unfortunately, if your attitude is anything less, there's nowhere it can hide.

Eye Contact. What are you hiding? Nothing? Good, then pass that message along as you speak to people and look them in the eye.

Leave Your "Problems" at the Office. Even if your office is just a corner of your home. Your family or friends should not have to suffer through hearing the story of your business difficulties when they want to enjoy your presence. Such conflicts of interest will make others wish you hadn't gone into business.

Pay Attention. May I have your attention please, while I am talking to you? No matter who is doing the talking or the listening, pay attention. Looking around while in a conversation conveys your lack of interest.

If I had no humor, I would long ago have committed suicide.

-Mahatma Gandhi

On Worrying

If you think you'll succeed by worrying about things, you'll continue to worry and use up all that energy and those creative juices in a do-nothing activity. Worrying takes more time and energy than planning, and it doesn't do a thing to take you off the hook if something goes wrong. If worrying makes you DO something, you would be doing it, and therefore eliminate the need to worry about it. Imagine how much more energy you'll have to actually DO those things you previously worried about instead. Don't let business become a worry-burden.

It's physically as well as emotionally draining, and its nonproductive. I know it is easy to say you won't worry, but hard to actually stay true to. Let's deal with some of the worries you will face:

- **I won't know something.** Okay, admit it and find out what you need to know.
- **I can't trust people.** Well, find reasons to trust certain people. If you must deal with someone you absolutely cannot trust, identify the reason behind it and then move forward cautiously. Remember, you can't change the spots on a leopard.
- **I won't be successful.** Start by acknowledging what success means to you. What does it look like? Picture yourself enjoying that kind of success. See yourself attaining it step-by-step. It costs you nothing extra to think positive.
- **They're all doing it better than I am!** Have you ever had a call from someone who wanted to come right over to see you at home, on your day off? This was the day you slept late, didn't do the dishes, were going to do the laundry, had your craft project all over the dining room table, and your hair was a mess!? Remember how you immediately went into action,

transforming your mess into a fairly organized home, and yourself into a ready-to-meet-your-public host? I hope you don't for one minute think that you're the only one who has never had to hide their dishes in the oven, or stuff things in a closet, or don sweatbands to have them think what you want them to think!

- **I can't stop worrying.** Well, ask yourself if there is anything you can do about what you are worrying about. If there is, do it. If there isn't, then just accept that that's life—which it is—and everybody shares this "I can't do anything about that" aspect of their personal and business lives. Sometimes, it is your own personal way of coping with or strategizing about things. It will help you to understand the element of being human that we all share. Take this story to heart and remember it's content when worry shrouds your life:

A man was pacing back and forth in his bedroom one night and his wife asked him what he was worrying about. He told her that he had a bank note due the next morning and he didn't have the money with which to pay it. He was distraught and in agony and could not sleep. The wife picked up the phone and dialed the president of the bank. When he answered, she explained about her husband and the note due the following morning. She told the banker that her husband did not have the money to pay the bank; therefore, he would not be in the next morning to pay the note! Upon hanging up the phone, the horror-stricken husband wanted to know why she had done that. She told him, "You do not have the money to pay the bank, you are upset and worried and cannot sleep. Now that he knows the truth, you can go to sleep and not worry. It's his problem now, and he can stay up and worry!

Do remember to add humor to your day because it is THE SPICE OF LIFE! I wish to first share a few book recommendations with you, and then some of my trusty truisms that will assist you in your humor exercises.

MY TOP TEN PICKS

1. Whining and Dining Your Way to Success
2. Dealing with Aggressive Timidity
3. How to Profit from Your "Mistakes"
4. You and Your Personal Trainee
5. Molding Your Employees' Behavior Through Guilt and Fear
6. Old Age and Treachery Will Overcome Youth and Skill
7. Simplifying Your Complexes
8. The Underachievers Guide to Very Small Business Opportunities
9. Achieving Self-Confidence Through Pretense and Ostentation
10. Business and the Art of Motorcycle Maintenance

TRUISMS

1. If at first you don't fail, be patient. You will eventually fail at something.
2. Ignore failure, and keep those ideas and inspirations flowing. Once you eliminate the ones that don't work, you'll be left with those that do.
3. Learn from your failures. You paid the price, now get more than your money's worth.
4. Play "the devil's advocate" by coming up with ideas that couldn't possibly work, and then looking for their merit. Who knows what you'll discover?
5. Be daring. Success happens one step at a time, but only if you keep marching.

Attitude, More Than Age, Determines Energy

There was never a time when there was more opportunity than today. We are living in the best of times, with all the information and technology at our fingertips, with the best yet to come. Our attitude at the beginning of a difficult task has more to do with the outcome than all the efforts we put into it. Life can't give you joy or success. Life only gives you time and space. It's up to you to fill it! It has been written that even the woodpecker owes his success to the fact that he uses his head and keeps pecking away until he finishes the job he starts!

Coping with Murphy

We can review Murphy's Law and take it under advisement. Part of business is going with whatever happens. Everything will go wrong—you expect it to go wrong. And when it does, hopefully you will have a sense of humor to assist your logical thinking and quick response to the situation. Attitude is half the battle of the action needed to be taken. The other half is how you react—what course of action you take—and learning from previous mistakes can prevent repeats by not doing the same "dumb" thing again.

Qualifying as a Professional

I define a professional as someone who answers positively to the following questions:

- Do you admit mistakes, do what you can to rectify the problem(s), and then learn from those mistakes, or do you blame others and/or cover up the mistakes?
- Are you a good listener (supportive, nonjudgmental), or do you insist on monopolizing the conversation by interrupting, criticizing or complaining, or offering your opinion when not asked?
- Do you respect the privacy of others, their right to their own style and opinions, or do you feel you're more important than they are and act

above the "rules," butting into their business, telling them how to look and think, and asking them personal questions?

- Are you committed to excellence, integrity, quality, and serving the needs of your customers, or do you prefer the easy way, however shoddy, and the big bucks without regard to value received?

- Do you have a winning attitude, or a whining attitude?

- Are you flexible, or do you demand something be done one way—your way—without regard for evaluation of what may be more efficient, better, or more workable for all concerned?

- Is your impressive title or position more important to you than your product or the service rendered to your customer?

- Can you be counted on in a pinch, or do you leave the tough stuff and the emergencies to others and walk away?

- Do you respect confidences, or do you not only tell secrets, but start and spread rumors, whether they're true or not?

- Are you able to see the big picture in running your business, or do you concentrate so much on tiny details that you could be seen as a nitpicker?

- Are you a team player who makes it a point to get along well with others, or do you tend to be a loner, making it impossible for others to know you, or work with you?
- Do you work at gaining your success through making your company "the best," or do you work at undermining the competition?
- When others around you move on to their own successes, are you genuinely happy for them? Or do you talk about them behind their backs, even though they think you're sincere in your congratulations?
- When involved in a disagreement, do you try to see the other person's viewpoint, or do you always have to be right?
- Do you proceed in building your dream because you really believe in it, or do you proceed only to make money or get famous, and hope that you'll eventually believe in what you're doing?

On Perfectionism

Perfectionism will wear you down and lead to fatigue rather than perfection. Our very nature, being human, makes it impossible for us to be perfect. Recognizing what's important and being flexible with the small stuff will make you seem like a more perfect person.

Let's try and solve this mystery. It is one that you could easily need to deal with as you start down the road to your business. What rule would you be breaking if:

- You seem to ignore your friends?
- You expect a lot more from your family or spouse?
- You work through lunch, past dinner, sometimes well into the night?
- You forget the meanings of vacation, time off, time out, spontaneity, coffee break, and fun?

Or:

- Your friends accuse you of losing your sense of humor?
- Your friends ask you if everything is all right at home?
- Your friends are calling less and worrying about you more?

ANSWER: The Cardinal Rule: you are not SUPERwoman, so don't overdo it. Lighten up! Allow the fun, sunshine, and joy back into your life. Remember, building your business from the dream up was supposed to enhance your life, not detract from it.

Who Am I?

I am your constant companion. I am your greatest helper or your heaviest burden. I will push you onward or drag you down to failure. I am completely at your command. Half the things you do, you might just as well turn over to me and I will be able to do them quickly and correctly.

I am easily managed; you must merely be firm with me. Show me exactly how you want something done, and after a few minutes I will do it automatically. I am the servant of all great men; and, alas, of failures as well. Those who are great, I have made great. Those who are failures, I have made failures.

I am not a machine, though I work with all the precision of a machine, plus the intelligence of man. You may run me for profit or run me for ruin—it makes no difference to me.

Take me, train me, be firm with me, and I will place the world at your feet. Be abusive with me and I will destroy you. Who am I?

PREPARING FOR YOUR SUCCESS

Leadership: For Yourself, for Others, for Business

...Only man, of all living things, foolishly strives to be other than what he was intended to be...You cannot choose your calling. Your calling chooses you.
  -Og Mandino, The Greatest Success in
                         the World

Managers Prepare for the Journey—Leaders Point the Way

To start your own business, it helps to be part manager, but the foremost requirement is to be a leader. It takes something more than being "average" or "capable" to be a leader. It requires willing people who are not afraid to work for what they want and possess the ability for self-motivation. It requires enthusiasm for completing tasks that others would walk away from and leave unfinished. It requires commitment, because the work will lead to long hours. It requires a positive mental outlook that will sustain through the negative times and ignore the pernicious behind-the-back talk. It requires a will to succeed.

Leaders possess the single extra heartbeat that differentiates them between success and failure. The little things they don't mind, like an extra hour, the extra call, the backbone to disagree even if it goes against the grain. The great difference between the powerful leader and the feeble leader is energy. Energy creates determination and purpose that will see any task to completion. It creates talent in any circumstance and it sees opportunity in the smallest of offerings.

Leadership is learned by those who truly want to be leaders, who feel it deep inside, and are willing to bear what goes with it. There is no exact science or method to explain entirely how leadership is learned. Leadership, like life, can only be learned as you go along. The ability to lead and inspire others is far more instinctual than premeditated, and it is acquired somehow through the experiences of one's everyday life. The personality and character of a leader is reflected in her ability to handle and deal with circumstances that surround events, whether they be normal or abnormal. Every woman has her own style of leadership, but it is the talents realized by each individual that determine the extent that she will use them.

At some point in your life and career you will discover that money is not all that matters (maybe you have already discovered this). You will learn the value of the experience offered, the challenge to test your own mettle, and also the fun, the enjoyment, the pride, and the self-fulfillment that rising to meet the challenge can bring to your inner being. To have reached the goal, to have a plan come together, to have outwitted someone in a competitive arena, to achieve the personal and professional victory that competing and winning can bestow—these are the rewards that cannot be bought.

Leadership is practiced not so much in words as in attitude and actions. No one wants a leader to be tolerant of incompetence, either through ignorance, indecisiveness, or weakness. No one wants to follow, much less respect, a weak leader. The leader sets the pace. The climate control is in the hands of the business owner who sets the temperature and quality of the air within the business. Much more respect and loyalty is given to the leader who is considered decent, fair, and reliable in dealing with the employees, and has the ability to "handle" daily business affairs.

The leader must research and compile the facts of any situation affecting the company and its growth. Knowledge is power, and facts supply the oxygen to knowledge, which provides for the total well-being of the company. They will provide indications of what you can expect to see, feel, or meet once you enter that particular segment of your company. It is important that you do not ignore facts that are indicators, or become complacent, accepting the status quo. This type of passivity could ultimately cause the downfall of your business. Standing on one leg and resting on your laurels is not the way to keep a company growing. It takes standing on both legs, without props, excuses, or placing blame on others.

The difference between ordinary and extraordinary is that little extra. Take your highest talents to their fullest measure. Your dream is counting on you! Move at your own pace and in your own way, but apply your character in the building process. Naturally, no one else can create your character for you. No one is supposed to. Although others may point the way, and even help define the objectives, the position of being the owner of the business, the work that goes with it, the responsibility factors, and therefore the joy belong to you. Let work and time confront each other and make an effectual blend with the faith that your successes will reach their highest potential, and yes, the promise. Be careful not to conflict or compromise your sincerity at any level. Others will feel your genuine interest and even your confidence if you will follow where your enthusiasm leads.

As the leader, you naturally inherit the responsibility of making the major decisions. It's the turf that goes with the position. First, it is important to control circumstances instead of being mastered by them; in other words, meet all situations with strength and act in accordance with rational, intelligent thinking. You can enjoy wonderful success, or feel the rough ride on the steep downward slope as a result of those decisions you must make when duty calls.

Most of the time you are going to make the right decisions; the good will out number the bad. You will be able to help others who work within your organization become more effective and productive in their areas of work by following your example. Everyone watches the leader! If you concentrate on making your leadership successful, you will create a momentum within the company which nurtures others and enriches feelings of pride and commitment. The energy levels will increase, producing results that you never dreamed possible.

Your employees are your first line of feedback. They will know what kind of leadership you show, and believe me, they **will** judge you. Strong leadership has a tendency to "pull" others aboard. Your employees will want to help and want to see you succeed. Your success is their success!

Most of your decisions will require interactions with others. The human relationships will be the key to how those interactions take place. When dealing with others, I like to remember the ten key elements of human relations.

TEN COMMANDMENTS OF GOOD HUMAN RELATIONS

1. Speak to people. Silence is golden when appropriate, but the sweet silver sound of a salutation is a spoken...

2. Smile. It's easier on your face, too, since it takes about five times as many muscles to frown as it does to

smile. And while you're smiling…

3. Call people by name. It is music to their ears, and makes you seem to…

4. Be friendly. If you really want friends, you must be aware of your interactive demeanor and…

5. Act cordial. Speak and act as if the world is watching, and…

6. Show an interest in people. You can enjoy each other's company more, and they'll feel good, especially if you can…

7. Be generous with praise and stingy with criticism. Yet, be honest with both, in order to…

8. Be considerate of the feelings of others. You will likely inspire the same toward yourself, making it easy to…

9. Respect the opinions of others. Consider there are at least three sides to a controversy: yours, the other person's, and the side that would resolve the issue, so…

10. Be alert to keeping peace and helping others. Having your own way and everything you want at the expense of hurting and shunning others is too big a price to pay, no matter how "successful" you are.

Well said.

> *You cannot bring about prosperity*
> *by discouraging thrift. You cannot*
> *strengthen the weak by weakening the*
> *strong. You cannot help the wage earner*
> *by pulling down the wage payer. You*
> *cannot further the brotherhood of man*
> *by encouraging class hatred. You cannot*
> *keep out of trouble by spending more than*
> *you earn. You cannot build character and*
> *courage by taking away man's initiative*
> *and independence. You cannot help men*
> *permanently by doing what they could*
> *and should do for themselves.*
> -Abraham Lincoln

CHAPTER FOUR

PREPARING THE WORKPLACE FOR SUCCESS

> *Old houses mended, Cost little less than*
> *new before they're ended.*
>
> -Colley Cibber

Humble Beginnings

There are a few things to toss around while you're making your fundamental decisions and plans for the future growth of your company. From humble beginnings, many successful businesspeople have launched multimillion dollar companies from their homes, garages, and basements! You may eventually reach the point, depending on the type of business you're in, when more and more clients begin to consistently come to you, and on that basis alone the situation will dictate the need for a more convenient location and a more professional atmosphere. Starting out at home, at least to begin with, is often an economical consideration or a personal, practical solution. Whatever the motives, I have listed some advantages and disadvantages of working at home. Later, when business dictates (and you will know when), you will need to consider a different type of atmosphere for your growing business. If money and/ or personal obligations are not the chief concerns, and a more professional image is, then a commercial building may be more suited to your needs to start with. Start off on the right foot, choose your workplace, by design or default, and begin creating the working atmosphere that best suits you.

THE GREAT EXCHANGE FOR WORKING AT HOME

Advantages	Disadvantages
Save on commuting time	Atmosphere too comfortable
Save on commuting expenses	Spreading out so much that there is no sense of focus or organization
Save on associated office expenses	Isolation from the flow/ hubbub of business
Save on eating out	Family, friends, neighbors, or pet distractions
No problem with inclement weather	Need to be totally self-motivated
Easier to set up and—if necessary—tear down	Need self-restraint regarding the frig and TV
Comfortable and familiar atmosphere	Easy to oversleep, start late, nap, or quit early
More control over who comes to your place of business	Procrastination—no real beginning or end to day

No matter where you decide to make your workplace, you are the boss, and as such you must be careful not to fall into the trap of losing the professionalism that is required. It is easy to say to yourself that you can come in a little late and leave a little early. Whether you are your only employee or if you have many working for you, the result is only negative. Your lack of consistency will be seen by others as unprofessional. Your inability to manage yourself will taint others in your organization. This is a business, and it's important to maintain a certain standard of professionalism for a business to be successful. Below are a few habits to try and avoid.

Zoning

When you select the business location, make sure the zoning is appropriate for the business. Every business should operate in a location that is zoned for the type of business to be performed at that location. Once the business complies with the zoning rules, it can receive a permit and business can start. Before you begin to move forward, ask yourself:

- Who can operate the business?
- How much space can you use?
- What kind of businesses are allowed?
- Do you need a zoning permit?
  Special use permit? A variance?

Then, gather the information that you will need. Be sure to send for your free local zoning packet from your city or county office. The packet should explain any unique rules that apply to your local zoning. It is important that you have the correct zoning permit for the area you plan to work in. There are several zoning-related offices that you may need to contact:

- Chamber of Commerce
- Local Planning Commission
- City or County Zoning Board
- Secretary of State

Typically, there are four zoning areas:

1. Residential—Working where you live
2. Commercial—Where you go to work
3. Industrial—Working where it's all work
4. Agricultural—Pretty much an open field

Be advised that many people operate home businesses without a permit. Of those who do get permits, many are not aware of the need for the additional "special use" permits. Of those who are aware, many never get them. What should you do? Read the zoning information contained in the free packet. You'll know what to do.

Zoning Variances—Official permission granted to do something normally forbidden by the zoning code. Talk to the people with your local zoning board. To check on any other existing restrictions, contact the secretary of state. Request the latest update on federal regulations regarding home businesses. Homeowners Association Restrictions—If you plan to work from your home and if you live in a home controlled by a Homeowners

Association, read the deed. Do NOT assume anything. Check and re-check the codes, covenants, and restrictions of the neighborhood before you act.

IRS Considerations and Stipulations—Send for a free booklet on home business space. Check your needs and considerations against their stipulations for authorized business deductions. It is best to know the tax laws before you commit. For any other restrictions, contact the secretary of state.

Success is a journey, not a destination
-Unknown

A Business Without a Sign Is a Sign of No Business

As simple as it may sound, your business needs a sign and one that accurately indicates what the exact nature of the business is. Have you ever noticed businesses with a name out front and you wondered, silently or out loud, "Just what is The Tie Down Inc.?" If you're going to have a name that does not reflect the nature of the business, at least expound with a slogan or explanation of what the business is about. It will certainly help the business, not hinder it.

Making Your Daily Routine Easier

Concentrate on condensing errands and making fewer trips to anywhere by getting the most out of the trips you do make. You will save yourself considerable time, energy, aggravation, and money. Examples: When at the post office, buy stamps by the roll. Pick up both the hard and soft Priority Mail envelopes for pre-addressing, as well as certified mail pieces if you send mail this way often.

Always take the time to make up your schedules— both business and personal. Having a schedule saves more time than the time it takes to make one. Put a value on your time!

The Centers of Attention

Chances are, you'll have just one area that's going to be your center of attention. It'll be your telephone center, your mail center, your financial center, and possibly even your filing center. It's called your desk! Your desk area will have many functions to contend with:

> THE MAIL CENTER: Needs to include some designation for incoming and outgoing, letter opener, your stationery, envelopes, stamps, postcards, note cards, U.P.S. or Federal Express mailing envelopes and their appropriate paperwork, business cards (to include with letters and mail-outs), large mailing envelopes, a stapler, and paper clips.

> THE TELEPHONE CENTER: Your phone, answering machine, fax machine, telephone message book with carbonless copy, a rolodex, and a card file.

THE MESSAGE CENTER: Perhaps a bulletin board by the door, with colored pushpins to simplify message-leaving for everyone in the workplace. Make it a habit to check it any time you've been out of the office, and before you leave for the day.

THE MONEY CENTER: Your invoices, bills, statements, records, receipts, tax returns, checks; your computerized financial program, accounting system, and petty cash fund. Your credit cards and other cash should remain with you, in your wallet, or locked in a very secure place.

THE FILING CENTER: A filing cabinet with files marked by colors or labels. Schedule a designated time to go through your "in" basket every day (I speak with the voice of experience!). There are many things you can do with paper: you can read it, act on it, file it, hide it, throw it away—just don't leave it in your "in" box as a permanent fixture.

SORTING SUGGESTIONS: When you do get items in your basket, sort them. Keep them organized so that you know which ones are urgent and which ones are for information only. I suggest using stackable shelf trays labeled:

- Requiring Action—with subcategories of:
  - To call
  - To write
  - To check on
  - To send for
  - To notate—on a calendar. Try using colored Post-it notes for attaching a quick description of the action and when it is needed by. Example: Ann, before Friday, zoning brochures; Brad, thank-you note.
- To be read
- To be filed
- To be paid

At the time of sorting, highlight the key word that something will be filed under, to save even more time when you get to the filing step. Be sure things are filed as conveniently as possible, and that your file labels clearly reflect your intention of retrieval. As files become useless, or of no current value, transfer them to an "inactive" file or to storage. Keep a directory of those inactive files to save hours of searching.

SAFETY INSPECTION CHECKLIST

- Do not overload outlets with too many plug-in items.
- Use surge protectors (electrical outlet strips) for all computer equipment.

- Turn off all equipment not being used when you leave the office or if you will not be using it for long periods of time.
- No matter how good your memory is, a reminder note on or near the exit door to turn off such and such will be worth its weight in uranium if you need it even once.
- Cultivate a "think safety" habit everywhere you look:
  - Are there wires or cords that someone could trip on?
  - Is that vase likely to go flying if someone slams the door?
  - Is the exit clear all the way to the outside?
  - Are you using defective equipment—nursing it along—because you can't afford to replace it? (Consider the cost of a fire, an injury or a death, a lawsuit).
  - Do you have the appropriate and required fire extinguishers, checked and approved by the fire inspector?
  - Have smokers been advised of where NOT to smoke and where NOT to put out their cigarettes?
  - Do you have smoke detectors and a sprinkler system, all in working

order, in the appropriate places?
Do you have spare batteries
nearby for the smoke detector?

STANDARD CHECKLIST FOR EACH DESK, INCLUDING YOUR OWN
(A DAILY QUIZ)

Do I thoroughly understand my role in this organization? If so:

- What is my top priority today?
- Which project will give me and/or the company the greatest gain for the time spent?
- Which project or task will cause me and/or the company the greatest distress if it does not get done?
- Is there anything left over from yesterday's list that needs attention?
- Is there something that has not been considered that will help me do a better job, help our company be more successful, and further better relations between all involved in making this business run?
- Am I sufficiently motivated to do my best today and pass that feeling on to others? (If the answer is no, go immediately to the "Inspiration Jar.")

A Woman's Companion—Inspiration Jar: A clear glass jar that contains pieces of folded-up paper, each one bearing a different inspirational or motivational message, such as:

- Smile. It makes others wonder what you've been up to.
- Behold the turtle. He makes progress only when he sticks his neck out.
- If at first you succeed, try to hide your astonishment.
- When life gives you lemons, make lemonade.
- Of all the things you wear, your expression is the most important.

Business Briefs for the Workplace

> *Make everything as simple as possible, but not more so.*
>
> -Albert Einstein

Company Image

Does anything about your business (the company colors, the logo, the business office, receptionist, secretary, salespeople, product itself, etc.) intimidate or send out the wrong message to others? Are you, as the person-in-charge/owner/founder of this business, seeing your business as the general public would if coming in contact with it for the first time, from telephone contact, to in-person contact, to buying and using the product or service? If you cannot be objective or "fair" in such evaluations, "hire" someone to act as a customer to get this important information for you.

Controlling Quality of Product and Service

Be sure "Quality Control" is in somebody's job description. Although you may not be able to control product perfection 100 percent, you should be able to offer customer service perfection. What your employees/ company representatives say and do is every bit as important as the actual product or service offered. Yet, even though 100 percent product perfection may be next to impossible, get as close to it as possible, and don't settle for excuses! Important note to remember: Of the "big three"—quality, speed, and cost—remember that you can most likely only get two. Choose carefully.

Research, Development and Production

If better is possible, good is not enough. Research and development costs are one thing; manufacturing the researched and developed product is another cost consideration. When doing research for one thing, don't overlook surprises and discoveries about something else.

Consider the packaging costs or the advertising costs to get your product or service to the public. Does the package cost more to produce than the product itself? Research and development may keep you ahead of the competition and save your business from future extinction. In business, things will, and do, constantly improve, whether it is customer service, advertising ingenuity, or the product itself. Be ready and always looking to the future.

Freight Expense

The charges you, the shipper, incur when you hire a transportation company (or a carrier) to ship your goods for you, whether it be by truck, train, airplane, boat, U.P.S., USPS, Federal Express, etc. Rates vary and there may be an extra charge for pick-up and delivery, or a large volume minimum. It is wise to call MANY companies before deciding on one.

Freight Bill or Bill of Lading

This is a pre-billing form that is rendered by a common carrier at the time of pick up. The form should have information written on it, such as point of origin of the freight, the name of the shipper, the name of the freight company, identification (how many) and description of the freight, its weight, and the amount of the charges. The number at the top of the form is known as a "tracking number." This is used in locating the shipment while it is in transit. You will learn the value of the numbers if you use freight transportation of any kind. They are known as "way bill" numbers, "tracking" numbers, "bill of lading" numbers, etc. Whatever the term used, have the numbers handy. Nowadays, you can track the shipment yourself via the Internet and the shipper's Website.

Bar Codes

The Universal Product Code (UPC) is a symbol placed on products and packaging (shipping containers) in the form of bars, referred to as bar codes. The system was originally designed for supermarkets, but is now used in every business across the country.

The symbol representations (bars) are read by electronic scanning systems usually at check-out. The products are passed over an optical scanner which reads the UPC symbol, decodes it to the UPC code number, and transmits this code number to a computer, which stores price and other information on all products sold in the store. The computer transmits back to the check-out stand the item's price and description, which are instantly displayed and printed on the customer's receipt tape, as well as sending relevant information on taxability, food stamp acceptance, etc. At the same time, the computer captures and stores information such as product movement, inventories, and sales, which is then merged and consolidated into an array of control reports that are beneficial to manufacturers, wholesalers, and retailers.

The UPC is a voluntary product-identification system that is provided by the product manufacturer. If you sell any kind of a product and your goals are to grow and expand, you will most definitely need to obtain your own UPC symbols. If you need additional information, go to their Website www.gs1us.org.

On Customers

An average company loses about 20 percent of its customers every year, and it costs five times as much to attract a new customer as to keep existing ones. The easiest, most inexpensive way to increase profits is to keep present customers while adding to the customer base.

A complaint does not mean the end of that customer's business if it is handled correctly and swiftly. If someone doesn't complain, that does not mean they're satisfied either. Make it easy for customers to complain so you can learn what you need to improve. Your customer retention and profits depend on it.

Take into account customers' expectations for your product or service, and list in order of importance according to a customer poll: reliability, durability, easy maintenance, ease of use, known or trusted brand name, low price, customer service, etc. Consider a follow-up with the customer who buys your product or service. Send a postage-paid card with questions regarding their satisfaction and ask that it be mailed back to you after they have used your product or service. This can be a very effective way to track your "market research" at the source. It also engenders good public relations with your customers. They will more likely stick with a product or service that they can comment on and critique than one that never asks their opinion. Let customer satisfaction (or dissatisfaction) be your best source of "market research" on an ongoing basis.

Don't be misled by the idea that you need to serve a great many people. If you serve a small segment of the population very well, and consistently, other customers will find you!

On Suppliers

Do not automatically believe that every business you do business with is honest—or dishonest. Every business is made up of the product or service and all the many people involved in getting that product or service to the public. One person's dishonesty does not make a company dishonest, nor does one person's integrity improve a shabby product or service. Consider the whole, and bring YOUR complaints—and compliments—to the attention of THEIR managers.

"A man may work from sun to sun, but a woman's work is only worth $.59 on the dollar."
- Unknown female comedian (of course!)

"There is a big difference between surviving (not going out of business) and making a profit."
- Barbee

On Profits and "Sales"

Profit cannot be had without successful sales of your product or service. It is necessary for you to first visualize, and then conceptualize, your product or service. Who are you trying to reach? Is it a large enough market to support your vision of success? Can you see the big picture?

Familiarize yourself with trends in the economy and with particular business fluctuations. Get in harmony with the ebb and flow of the profit picture. Create a powerful plan to put "punch" behind your product and substance behind your service. Look for affordable advertising for your specific market.

Identify and utilize your many resources when powering up your business plan. Collect customers even before you open shop. Put your energy up-front, as opposed to after the fact. Make all your efforts count. "A stitch in time saves nine."

Let customer satisfaction be the automatic pilot that will guide you to the "Port of Profits." Do unto others… (and that doesn't mean before they do unto you).

Let your business soar to its own heights, at its own rate, as you continually guide it and readjust it according to market trends. "Haste makes waste."

Ride the wave and go with the flow, overcoming obstacles and handling the hurdles as they appear. Keep "failures" and "problems" at a manageable level by not having any one aspect of your business bring down all the other aspects in a crash. The old "Don't put all your eggs in one basket" theory applies.

Accept success and profits, adjusting your business plan as you go along when necessary to accommodate the big picture. Grow with your business. In business, as in life, all things change with time. Increase your skills and knowledge constantly!

On Scheduling

Avoid scheduling anything that conflicts with time or transportation arrangements. Just because your first meeting will end at two o'clock doesn't mean you can make it to your next meeting at two thirty if it's clear across town.

Don't fill up your calendar with appointments that can be taken care of with phone calls or letters. Remember your priorities and schedule your family activities first, so as to not forget to show up for that important teacher conference or family reunion.

Afternoon Tea

As an alternative to the cocktail hour, plan afternoon tea around three or four o'clock, in order to discuss whatever you would normally discuss over cocktails or dinner. Less fattening, less expensive, less time-consuming, and perhaps more business will get discussed. Tea is a pleasant substitute for cocktail parties and sets a different tone for expressing YOU.

Philanthropy/Philosophy

Decide in advance on your philanthropy, your charity-giving policy. Write it up. Be sure everyone in your organization knows it and uses it. You WILL be approached by solicitors for your money. Have an alternate way of giving—perhaps SERVICE.

Holidays—Celebrating—Donations—Giving

Sooner or later, every business is faced with certain thrust-upon-them choices: Do we recognize and/or celebrate Christmas in the workplace? What about other specialty holidays (those that are identified with decorations and special sales tie-ins)? What about donating to the various charities and good causes that are sure to find you now that your shingle is hung and you're open for business?

Deciding your policy in advance will make your business life less stressful at holiday times and more joyful all year round. What you decide now does not have to be engraved on your walls, it can be "painted over" and changed as your situation requires, or you change your mind.

Considerations

Regardless of the various meanings behind it, Christmas is the biggest holiday of the year, having its very own "selling season." If you identify with Christmas as a religious holiday, you may or may not reflect that in your decorations. If you enjoy the secular festivities of the season, your workplace will probably reflect your creative Christmas spirit. Yet personal preferences aside, the Christmas season is always a bigger buying season, and you are now a businesswoman with something to sell. Without compromising your principles, can you see a way to promote your product or service as a gift to give others? Can you add "Christmas cheer" to your place of business? Will it hinder or help you sell?

It is also at Christmastime that you will most likely be approached for "extracurricular" giving. People will call; they'll mail you letters of solicitation; they may show up at your door. Avoid that awkward feeling of what to say when you not only can't give, but really don't want to.

If you develop a policy that clearly states your feelings about how, what, and/or to whom you give, all you need do is state it for all solicitors. Then give them a hearty "Merry Christmas," "Feliz Navidad," "Joyeux Noel," or whatever suits your spirit best!

Remember the M & M's

Remember to create or select a MOTTO or slogan to represent your intention in this new venture, or your source of strength. Read it and say it every day.

Remember to compose your MISSION STATEMENT, the motivation of your whole venture into the business world. Post it not only for yourself but for customers as well. Let everyone know why you are in this business, and how you intend to make the world a little better.

Recycling—Waste Not, Want Not

- Show you care about the environment and the planet. Insist on waste management, recycling, conservative use of supplies, and using recyclables instead of disposables. Lead by example. Be aware of everyday usage of supplies.
- Recycle locally anything that can be used again:

  Paper and cardboard boxes
  Mailing boxes
  Large envelopes
  Plastic containers
  Aluminum
  Glass
  Printing cartridges

Where to recycle? Need a little help? Try these for starters and expand from your own research:
Computers—www.sharetechnology.org
Cell phones and rechargeable batteries—www.rbrc.org
Electronics—www.mygreenelectronics.org

Housekeeping

If everyone in the office took responsibility for the neatness and cleanliness of the general workplace, as well as their individual workspace/desks, only "heavy-duty" cleaning would be necessary: windows, carpet cleaning, bathroom sanitizing, etc. This would cut down on expenses and only take each person a few minutes each day to accomplish.

In and Out of the Workplace

There are many other things that are useful to note about running a business. Some of them include but are not limited to:

- Post operational directions step-by-step on pieces of equipment.
- Do not discuss business in front of strangers, in elevators, etc., or loud enough to attract attention in public.
- Strive for repeat business and ask for referrals.
- Create momentum: become self-generating and self-sustaining.
- Remember: It's not what you save, it's what you SPEND that will be reflected on the bottom line.
- Become a notary, have one of your employees become one, or locate one near your office.
- Do not sign copies before you photocopy them unless you are absolutely sure that they are suitable for your purpose. Some places will need to see you sign all copies.

- Break the mold of usual thinking patterns; try creative thinking and brainstorming.
- When nervous, perhaps at a meeting or when giving a speech, use the old "imagine them picking their noses" ploy to make you feel more relaxed, or at least keep you smiling.

The Internet and Your Business

Creating a Website

First of all, a Website is a necessity and customers expect it! It needs to be used like a pack-mule, full of useful information and embellished with a good design that makes navigating through it easy and fulfilling. The trick is to make sure your Web plans are compatible and fully communicate your marketing message and business image. Depending on your budget, you can incorporate high technology, music, multimedia, and interactive elements to show your business off!

Hire It Out or Do It Yourself

It's possible to provide a little do-it-yourself with some paid services and still end up with an attractive, professional, and interesting-looking Website that is up and running quickly. Sure, there are software packages out there to help you design and build your own Website, you just have to find the right one! At this writing, some leading programs include Microsoft Expressions (www. microsoft.com, $300-$600) and Adobe Dreamweaver (www.adobe.com, $400). Browse online and find who built the sites you like (Guru.com). They let you post your project and get quotes for the work. Marketingtool. com lets you find Website designers in individual states, like where you live.

With a little technical assistance, anybody can create a Website that will attract potential customers. With a mid-sized budget ($500-$1,000), you can hire an experienced Web designer to build your site and keep it updated for a few hundred dollars per year.

Website hosting can be explained as renting space on a company's computer server for your Website. The domain name registration may be an additional minimal fee per year. Some Web hosting companies to research: Yahoo Small Business (http://smallbusiness.yahoo.com, click on "Web Hosting"), FatCow (www.fatcow.com), and Homestead (www.homestead.com).

Expect to get custom graphics or nicely designed templates to choose from, which include easy navigation starting with the main page, explanation of how they will optimize graphics and content for fast loading, and, of utmost importance, make sure you own the registration of the site and domain name.

Options and More Options

Google has an online marketing program with cost per click pricing that lets you control how much you want to spend each month (http://adwords.google.com) and will display your Website targeted to relevant search results.

Yahoo! Local (http://local.yahoo.com) has a featured listing program that can help you tap into a local customer base. Pricing starts at $25 per month at this writing.

For a deeper knowledge regarding the world of selling via the Internet, look for the most recently written books on the subject of creating Websites. There are a couple of books at this writing to check into if you're considering business on the Internet. The first is *Internet Commerce* by Andrew Dahl, Leslie Lesnick, and Lisa Morgan. This book gets into the details of electronic commerce solutions, including how to create your storefront and conduct business over the Web, and includes an overview of Internet commerce providers, cryptography basics, and Web server capabilities (New Riders; ISBN 1-56205-496-1).

The second is *Electronic Selling—23 Steps to E-Selling Profits* by Brian Jamison, Josh Gold, and Warren Jamison. This book is most helpful for learning the fundamentals of electronic commerce. It outlines the advantages, opportunities, and realities of conducting business on the Internet, plus an assortment of success stories (McGraw Hill; ISBN 0-07-032930-3). US West has published *Seven Things to Remember in Creating a Web Presence.* If you can overcome the technical aspects, or have savvy friends who can help you, this is definitely an avenue to explore.

Your Website Should Have Basic Necessities

The content of the "Main Page" should include your company name, what you do, where you're located, your hours of operation, contact information, a list of your products, and a "virtual shopping cart" for online buying, if applicable. Keep the required information as basic as possible in any online form you require the customer to fill out to order your product or services. You can lose potential clients by asking for too much information and requiring that they fill in too many fields. Minimal and easy navigation is essential, so visitors can find what they want within seconds of clicking on to your site. Otherwise, they may leave and never return.

By all means, research and contact different sources when you are considering the Website. It is important to know what you're talking about and how you want your business presence to look on the Internet; for instance, layout, graphics, easy navigation, and plenty of pages. You will want an easy-to-remember domain name (like www.yougogirl.com). Some registrars offer a free ad-supported Website with each domain registration. You can expect to pay a minimal fee per year to register your name. Some hosting providers will give you a free domain with purchase of a hosting package. See what I mean? Study up and know what you're talking about,

Reaching Beyond Ordinary

The marketing aspects of the Internet are enormous. Remember that the content of your site and links to your site from other Websites are important factors in search engines that can favor your site if done properly. These are known as "Tag" words. Search engines look for keywords like "Consulting" or "Las Vegas" to figure out where your site fits. It's a useful tool to get listed with sites that have city guides or directories for your area. Local newspapers' sites can be a great source and Yahoo! Local (http://local.yahoo.com) is one free resource.

Grabbing Customers Is What It's All About

The idea is to get repeat visitors/customers to your Website. This alone can be challenging. Therefore, a regularly updated photo gallery of your wares or services and updated Blogs (a form of writing a daily, weekly, or monthly column via your Website) will give potential and established customers a reason to visit and return to your Website. You might even consider giving incentives such as coupons available online only. Bottom line is— nothing beats having current content!

Let Them Find You

Women are spending millions of dollars online each year, and this means that the Internet is a very exciting place to be right now because of its booming popularity. Geography doesn't limit the distance your Website can travel; therefore, you may find yourself with customers from all over the world depending on your product or services. The main idea is to let them know you exist.

Will You Be Selling to the Government?

Consider Electronic Commerce. Our government is transforming and becoming as automated as we are by purchasing goods and services either through electronic commerce or credit card purchases. If you are unfamiliar in the area of doing business with the government, there are many resources you can tap into for education and assistance, such as the Procurement Outreach Programs, Minority Purchasing Councils, and the SBA. Each agency hosts seminars and workshops specifically targeted to vendors, private contractors, and the governmental agencies. You can also dial into the ECRC (Electronic Commerce Resource Center) in Oakland, California, to find a centralized place where all of the government sites can be accessed (http://www.oakland.ecrc.org).

Government Classification Systems

Be aware of the new classification system going into effect known as the "NAICS" (North American Industry Classification System). This is a new acronym that will be replacing the "SIC" industry classification system as the government moves closer to implementing a system of electronic commerce.

For those of you who already have an existing SIC classification (four digits), a new NAICS code (six digits) guide is available, and your company will simply have to change its classification codes. Others, such as consulting firms and analysis shops, specifically Dunn & Bradstreet, etc., will have to completely revise their entire data systems.

Individual product categories will increase from seven digits to eleven digits. You can see the new directory personally if you have Internet access (http://www.census.gov). Select "Subjects A-Z," "N," or "NAICS."

Government (Purchase Cards) VISA Cards

If you sell products that are typically under $2,500, the government is now issuing VISA cards (called IMPAC) that are limited to $2,500 per day (the minimums could change from the time of this publication), with a weekly or monthly cap. You may go directly to the SADBUS (Small and Disadvantaged Business Utilization Specialist) at each installation and they should be able to tell you who has the cards and who doesn't. This takes quite a bit of red tape out of a small business selling to the government, plus makes them more price-conscious and service-oriented.

CAGE Codes and the Procurement Outreach Programs

You will need a CAGE (Commercial and Government Entity) code to sell to the government. This is a discrete number assigned to your company, and it is used only for identification. If you don't have one, the Procurement Outreach Program (part of the government's Commission on Economic Development) in your area can assist you in getting one. You will need a CAGE code for bids, and to get paid! In other words, contact the Procurement Outreach Program specialists and work closely with them for your entrance and continued success in working with the government.

Collecting Your Money

The Buck Stops Here!
-Harry Truman's desk motto

The premise is simple: you have something to offer the public, for a particular price. You deserve—and are legally entitled—to be paid in exchange for your product or service. It is your duty to yourself and your company to collect what you are due.

Ways to Collect What You Are Due

While you may have the right to your payment, not everyone is willing to give it to you. In those hopefully rare cases, you will need to pursue that payment. There are many ways to solicit payment. In all cases, you need to try the most subtle approaches first and increase your fervor with every attempt. Try these:

- Ward off nonpayment by requesting payment at time of purchase. Cash is best. (Check bills for legitimacy.)
- If accepting credit cards, follow the credit card agency's system for verifying customer and card and credit authorization.
- If accepting checks, carefully check photo ID (current driver's license or passport); then, on the back of the check write down the driver's license number, expiration date, and date of birth. Always cross check the signature for authenticity.
- Do not let accounts go from month to month. Have a standard (form) reminder statement to send to anyone who is late after the first billing, another after the second, and a special pre-paid response for the third. Examples:

We know how easy it is to forget some things. We all do it. Your business is important to us, and we'd like to continue offering you the convenience of free short-term credit.
   - May we hear from you soon—with your payment?

Perhaps our envelopes crossed in the mail. If you've sent us your check, we thank you. If you haven't, please take a moment now to do so.

- We look forward to serving you again soon.

Perhaps you're having difficulty sending us the payment as you agreed to. If you anticipate a longer delay, please call or write us to make special arrangements.

- We've enclosed a pre-paid return envelope for your convenience.

If we do not hear from you, we are put in the position of having to make assumptions. Have you run off to Rio? Changed your name, address, phone number, identity? Decided to spend the money you were going to send on a new Harley? Still recovering from amnesia? Please let us know; otherwise, we will be compelled to let a collection agency stay on your trail.

- Offer incentives for paying on time. Offer a discount for payment at time of purchase. "We offer a 5 percent discount today for cash purchases. Will that be cash, or cash?"

Insurance Coverage and Finding the Right Agent

The insurance coverage that a business needs usually depends on the type of business it is and what areas of concern need to be insured. There are numerous policies to cover just about any aspect of any business, but the problem is in finding a credible insurance agent, and a credible insurance underwriter, one who will custom-fit the insurance policies to the business needs and keep you up-to-date at least once a year. There are policies offered that will cover business interruption, accounts receivable, malpractice, insurance for franchises and mail-order companies, bonding, and so forth.

In the search for an insurance agent, ask other business owners for personal recommendations. Ask your accountant. Ask those you know, respect, and trust for their opinions. You will need to discuss your business fully with the newfound insurance agent, so that she may be better able to advise you on specific coverage that best suits your business needs. Compare companies, policies (coverage), and costs very closely.

Bonding

Not the type you do with your family or friends, but the kind you purchase for your employees, if your business needs require it. The purpose of bonding an employee is for protection. There are different types of bonding that relate to different employment positions and duties.

Fidelity

Protects business owner against employee theft or embezzlement. A couple of categories fall under this heading:

1. Schedule Bonds—Lists all names and/or positions to be covered
2. Blanket Bonds—Covers all employees, but does not identify them by name or title, so no conflict occurs if hiring and firing takes place
3. Surety Bonds—Guarantees the employer that the employee will finish the job she was hired to do

If the above seems "fuzzy" to you in any way regarding insurance and policy types, after you have spoken to your agent, continue speaking with different agents until it becomes clear. Then, you will have discovered the real-life agent you can communicate with. Be sure the policy says the same things she says! If you need help in locating an agent or broker in your area, check the Internet for agencies, comparisons, and public opinions of companies and policies.

NOTE: Insurance brokers insure property and insurance agents insure people.

Now would probably be a good time for another dose of:

GRANDMA BARBEE'S
MINI BOOK OF QUOTES

Time is the most valuable thing a man can spend. -Diogenes

You can't win the prize if you don't take the chance.

One's best qualities shouldn't be measured by extraordinary circumstances but by everyday deeds. -Benjamin Franklin

Don't compromise yourself. You are all you've got. -Janis Joplin

Don't be a perfectionist about unimportant things.

Wisdom is priceless and cannot be stolen.

Good manners cannot cover up unkind words.

Let others speak of your accomplishments. It is enough that you accomplish.

Don't be afraid to have courage.

Youthfulness often comes with age.

All the money in the world can't buy the knowledge that comes from poverty.

Our real power lies in not having to use it.

Trying to prove one's strength can be a sign of weakness.

Never say never.

The end of something is only the beginning.

There is no work that cannot also be fun if you love it.

Nothing great was ever achieved without enthusiasm.
-Ralph Waldo Emerson, *Circles*

Our aspirations are our possibilities.

Be courageous! When you look back, you'll regret the things you didn't do more than the things you did.

CHAPTER FIVE

SALES, MARKETING, AND ADVERTISING

> *Nothing in the world can take the place of persistence. Talent will not, nothing is more common than unsuccessful men with talent. Genius will not; unrewarded genius is almost a proverb. Education will not; the world is full of educated derelicts. Persistence and determination alone are omnipotent.*
>
> -Calvin Coolidge

Secrets of Selling

If there truly were a secret to selling, some profit-seeking, financially able corporation would have bought it by now! Or, contrarily, some opportunity-seeking, career-changing employees would have packed the secrets up as they left one company and passed them on to their next company of employment to advance further up the ladder—quicker.

There are "keys" or "guidelines" we follow for successful selling that have common characteristics. The most important "secret to selling" is constant learning and training. With each new day there arrive new books, periodicals, seminars, speakers, and briefs that come into existence trying to capture the "secret" of the subject.

You could ask ten different people what their philosophies are on selling, and you would more than likely get ten different answers. Unequivocally, the most important "key" to successful selling is keeping up with what is new while never throwing out the tested, tried, and true of the old. The old never goes out of fashion in the selling world, and that same world welcomes the "new" with open arms. In the sales world there is always room for improvement, and it's cloaked with a kindred spirit of "sharing" when the new trends, information, technologies, and theories arrive. People naturally like to share knowledge with others, so talk about the sales world and attend helpful seminars.

K.I.S.S.

Successful salespeople know the key to closing a sale is in keeping things simple. It's called the "K.I.S.S." theory ("Keep It Simple, Silly"). They learn what benefits a customer wants and they find the products that have them. Example: If you're selling software and packages that contain the world, explain only a couple of products and their complex features in the simplest terms.

The Art of Selling

The art of selling begins with obliterating would-be negative thinking and instilling positive thinking. One of the greatest hindrances to selling is "fear." There is the fear of people, the fear of failure, and the fear of rejection. Fear imposes limitations on us with powers that erode our self-esteem, our self-confidence, our sense of self-worth, and leads us down the self-defeating path to immobilization. Fear tries to convince us we are unable to achieve, unable to attain, unable to succeed. As long as we allow fear to have a grip on us, we will never step up to the plate!

Franklin D. Roosevelt so eloquently said: "We have nothing to fear but fear itself." If you think you lack ability, talent, education, or initiative, and allow negative thoughts to fill your mind, and you buckle under the slightest amount of pressure along the way, then you'll not enjoy the sweet taste of victory because of fear.

To face our fears is to grow. To face the temporary setbacks, obstacles, disappointments, or even failures is to build character. To endure and conquer is success that has developed character and wisdom is what we develop and earn. Yes, it's a battle. Yes, it's difficult. Yes, it will be worth it when it's all said and done. No one can ever take that from you once you've earned it. In the words of a Roman centurion we find so much truth: "What does not conquer me only makes me stronger."

Women are overcomers! We have a history of being overcomers—read the history books! As we face the masked enemy, we confront our fears and we find it empowering.

If you are to succeed in your business, you cannot give up. Persistence is powerful. There will be setbacks and you will have to keep going. Don't dwell on the No's; instead, start looking to the next opportunity. You have a product or service to sell and, providing you believe that it is the best product or service, you can look at sales as your ability to offer something for others to benefit from.

Now This Is Perseverance!

If you've ever had any doubts that perseverance can overcome barriers or that success can follow adversity, consider the following "resume" of a famous politician:

'32 – Lost job; defeated for legislature
'33 – Failed in private business
'34 – Elected to legislature
'35 – Sweetheart died
'36 – Suffered nervous breakdown; ran for house speaker and was defeated
'43 – Defeated for nomination to Congress
'46 – Elected to Congress
'48 – Lost renomination
'49 – Ran for land officer and lost
'54 – Ran for Senate and lost
'56 – Defeated for nomination for Vice President
'58 – Lost election for Senate again
'60 – Elected 16th President of the United States
Abraham Lincoln!

The Bumblebee

Look at the bumblebee. In the world of physics, he is not aerodynamically designed to fly. His body is too heavy and his wings are too light. (Just imagine when he fills his jaws with the extra weight of pollen what that does to the physics phenomenon.) He doesn't have a fear of failure or a fear of not being able. He doesn't listen to negatives about his limitations. He just miraculously goes about his business very busily. There's a lesson to be learned here—let's get busy about our business!

Hit the Pavement Running

When you begin selling your products or services, "hit the pavement" (a term often used for selling with determination) and do it with enthusiasm and self-confidence. Believe you're going to make the sale, get the appointment, or land the new account! Here's an extra thought on sales calls.

One survey showed:

> 2 percent of sales were closed on the first call
>
> 3 percent of sales were closed on the second call
>
> 4 percent of sales were closed on the third call
>
> 10 percent of sales were closed on the fourth call
>
> 81 percent of sales were closed on the fifth call

There is no substitute for making sales calls.

Salespeople

Achievement in anything has a set of rules, just like the instructions that accompany any recipe (especially chocolate chip cookies). Follow the instructions step-by-step and you'll have a finished product of successfully baked chocolate chip cookies. Omit, substitute, or change one of the steps, and you're likely to have a bad baking day.

In sales, there are a set of guidelines to follow. Everyone in business knows that selling requires dedication and continuous follow-up. The skilled salesperson (we're talking about a unique personality here) knows it is a battle to get to the top and stay there. When the time comes that your business can afford it, you will want to hire the skilled and professional salespeople your company needs to grow and keep pace with the competition and the company's goals. The salespeople who represent your company in the field are a vital organ to the life of the company. It is important they thoroughly understand the philosophy and mission of the company they are not only working for, but representing. It is also important that you, the owner, know the type of personality that is representing your company on a daily basis to your present and potential customers.

Good salespeople are not easy to find, and great salespeople are even harder to find. If you are in business, eventually you will more than likely need salespeople. Look for someone that can sell your product/service with a high degree of honesty, imagination, and just the right amount of persistence. Remember, everyone has his or her own way to be a success. It's pretty much all an experiment; what works well for one may not work for another. The 80/20 rule applies: 80 percent of the sales will be brought in by 20 percent of the salespeople. Don't be surprised that everyone in your workforce will not achieve the same results.

> *The way to success is often through perseverance. Successful people see their failures as stepping stones; unsuccessful people see their failures as roadblocks.*
>
> Anonymous

What's "In" a Salesperson?

It's "IN" the way they look at things. One sees an acorn, another sees the giant oak tree. One sees a chunk of coal, another sees a beautiful diamond. One sees a vacant lot, another sees a piece of land where a beautiful building or structure could be built. One sees a desert, another sees an oasis in the desert—a gambling Mecca. One sees themselves with a "job," another sees themselves on the beginning rung of the ladder on their way to the top of a "vocation." One sees a barn filled with horse manure, another sees it as a barn that just has to have a horse nearby!

Some suffer from myopia. Their vision is too short. They don't see the big picture and have no business in the sales business. Contrarily, those whose vision is long-range are the real players.

Have you ever heard the old saying "you're known by the company you keep"? It's true, but it goes farther than that. Make certain they're the kind of people you are, or better still, the kind of people you would like to measure up to!

Two Frogs of a Different Nature

Let me tell you about two frogs who jumped into a bucket of cream on a dairy farm in Wisconsin.

"May as well give up," croaked one, after trying in vain to get out. "We're gonners!"

"Keep on paddling," said the other frog. "We'll get out of this mess somehow!"

"It's no use," said the first. "Too thick to swim. Too thin to jump. Too slippery to crawl. We're bound to die sometime anyway, so it may as well be tonight." He sank to the bottom of the bucket and died.

His friend just kept on paddling, and paddling, and paddling. And by morning he was perched on a mass of butter which he had churned all by himself. There he was, alive and full.

That little frog had discovered what most folks ignore: if you stick with the task long enough, you're going to be a WINNER!

Problems bring about possibilities. Establish it in your heart to believe that the contributors to inner strength are a confident spirit, a hopeful attitude, enthusiasm in the face of problems, and the determination to handle any situation that comes up. Don't let temporary setbacks set you back permanently.

If you are to succeed in your business, you cannot give up. Persistence is key. There will be setbacks and you will have to keep going. Don't dwell on the no's. If someone says no, you say, "Next!" and start looking to the next opportunity. You have a product or service to sell and there are people out there who need and want it. You must believe that it is the best product or service, and then you can look at sales as your ability to offer something to others that they will benefit from. All you can do is give others the opportunity to take advantage of your product or service. You must do everything in your power to make sure that you have given them ample information and/or a demonstration to make an informed decision—and then ask for the sale!

TEN COMMANDMENTS OF SELLING

I. KNOW THY STUFF: Learn all you can about your field or product/service, and the competition. No one knows your company like you do, but be prepared for a test of your knowledge.

II. UP THY ATTITUDE: You can often make up for a lack of knowledge or ability with a positive attitude. Desire and dedication will lead you to the necessary action.

III. MAKE THY FIRST IMPRESSION A GOOD ONE: Initial contact sets the tone for the business relationship. Every contact with every person is an opportunity to present who you are and what you are doing. Make a good impression. Spark interest. Notice interest. Be prepared to follow up on interest and encourage trust.

IV. GAIN RESPECT: Give everyone a feeling of confidence in you by the way you look, talk, and act. Do not put the competition down—simply show why you are better. Don't be cocky—be confident. Superiority shows, but let it speak for itself. Respect is earned, not bought or given on demand. You must appear, as well as be, worthy of their trust and respect.

V. BE ENTHUSIASTIC: Your business is an exciting adventure. You believe in it; you need to nurture it. People notice your energy level and your own belief in what you are doing. Don't be dull. If you can't be excited about your own project, how can you expect others to be? Plant the seeds of optimism and excitement, and watch them grow.

VI. BE WARM AND FRIENDLY: Make customers feel comfortable. Let your smiles be genuine. Show them you truly care about their needs.

VII. BE OPTIMISTIC: Believe in happy outcomes. Stir up customers' genuine interest in you by presenting desirable possibilities and creating positive images through your choice of "feel good" words.

VIII. BE LOW-KEY: Even though you are passionate about your business, avoid high-pressure tactics. Nobody likes heavy-handed high-pressure tactics, no matter how much you believe in what you are doing and how much you desire to make others see it as you do. Why use a fire hose to water the flowers when a garden hose will do the job? Use a low-key approach. It will increase your customers' confidence in you.

IX. BE QUIET: The most important thing about speaking is knowing when to close your mouth. Guide the conversation, don't monopolize it, and don't offer unnecessary information. You do not need to constantly add to what has been said.

X. BE AWARE: Notice the subtle signals that tell you your customer is ready to buy. Confirm such interest with pointed questions aimed straight toward making the sale. Ask for it, accept it, make the exchange, and thank them. If they offer, accept their unsolicited offer to give, invest, or buy.

More of Less

Once you have made the introduction of your products or services at the presentation meeting, it is time to move to the actual "sales pitch." That is, the unveiling of your product or passing out the literature you have prepared. You should have a proposal ready that clearly states what your company is about and the product or service your company is offering: the pricing structure, quantity, delivery time, and any other special arrangements your particular business may require, briefly stated. Once the presentation is finished and questions have been answered, be careful not to overstay your time allotted for the meeting. Do not oversell your products or services by rambling on with unending statements; it is a sign of nervousness. Answer any question straight to the point. Businesspeople like to have their questions answered and their concerns explained. Then, move on. The objective is to **ask for the business** and finalize a business transaction.

It is better to come across mannerly, courteous, knowledgeable, and professional in the beginning. There will be plenty of time to chit-chat and become a "friend" or a "good old' gal" when you have the business and it becomes prove-yourself time. It is then that you want to have a more comfortable working relationship with your customers; one where they feel comfortable to call you at any given time and you will be there to answer more questions, or better yet, be there for them with customer service after the deal is done. The "business relationship" is another one of those important elements to keeping a customer happy.

For much more help in these areas, be a regular in your favorite library or book store and read, read, read! This book is a guide to pointing you in the right direction, getting you safely there, and giving you fabulous advice along the way. It is not the end of the journey! You need to continuously attend selling seminars, join tips clubs, and it would be especially nice to find a mentor who is an already established success in the field of sales. That's what successful and confident salespeople do...they keep on going until they're ready to pull it all in and just consult or travel (I think, I'm not sure....I'm not finished myself yet!).

Catchy Phrases to Throw Around in the Sales Game Arena

Probably since the beginning of time, or at least sales, people have used some of these same phrases to help close a sale. Some actually work. Check them out for yourself.

- Try it yourself
- Check around, check our competitors
- No risk—our word is our bond
- We stand behind our claims
- Your family/friends will be thrilled
- I wish I had it years ago
- See for yourself
- Our product/services speak for themselves
- We're new; try us, you'll like us
- Our supply is limited
- Buy now—save BIG
- Buy one (or two) and get one FREE
- Free gift if you buy (order) NOW
- Buy before the price increase and save
- 100 percent satisfaction guaranteed!

Find It, Face It, Fix It—The Weak Link

A business is only as strong as its weakest link. No matter how much effort and money you pour into making your product (or service) the best, if your sales staff is rude, lazy, or inattentive, it's obvious that your business will suffer. If your suppliers are undependable or lacking in knowledge, it is possible that your business will again suffer. You need to do something quick—like do it yourself—until you get a better salesperson, and while you're at it, get a better supplier. A dishonest salesperson does not turn honest by getting caught. Give no second chances for deliberate dishonesty. Dishonesty is not a mistake; it's a decision.

What Customers Really Want

To Our Customers

YOU are the most important people we serve.

YOU deserve our attentive and courteous treatment.

YOU do not interrupt us; you are the purpose for our being here.

WE want you to depend on us; we must depend on you.

WE ask that you tell us if you have any complaints, and tell your friends and acquaintances if you're satisfied.

WE hope you'll be back.

Great Salespeople Are Self-Made...With A Little Help

Dignity...You Were Born With It!

A series of reverses had deprived him of money, possessions, and finally of self-respect. He turned despairingly to begging—extending an unsure hand with a few pencils in it at subway stations in downtown Manhattan.

One day, an elderly banker dropped a quarter in the beggar's trembling hand, turned to go, hesitated, and then wheeled on the mendicant with, "I want to apologize for treating you as a beggar. You are a merchant, of course, and I came back for the pencil I paid for." The astonished peddler handed the banker five pencils and thanked him with wondering warmth. Many months later, the banker stopped in a small stationery store on the outer fringe of the Wall Street area. As he was about to leave after making a few minor purchases, the proprietor stopped him and said, "I'm certain you won't remember me, but I will never forget you. Some time ago, I was a subway beggar with a handful of pencils and you treated

me as a businessman—a 'merchant,'
you called me. That comment gave me
back my self-respect. From then on, I
refused gifts and really sold pencils…
lots of them, and good ones too! From
this sidewalk business I saved my
money, borrowed a bit more, and then
opened this little shop. I'm beginning
to make a go of it, and all because of a
few kind words from you."

Marketing

Effective marketing consists of several key elements
that allow you to pursue your customers with a well-
thought-out method. They include:

- Market research
- Distribution channels
- Pricing
- Advertising/promotions/publicity
- Selling

Competition and Contribution

Compare yourself to the competition, but only to show
how you are better, not to tear them down. Having their
products around will help. Don't have your prices so low
that you make no profit. That is insulting to your hard-
working body and your creative and dedicated spirit (to
say nothing of your hard-working employees), and only
reinforces a "scarcity" mentality. Be competitive in price,
but surge way ahead in quality. You <u>know</u> you're better
than your competition or you wouldn't be dreaming of

putting yourself out there in that way. After tasting the <u>best</u> cookies, do you go out of your way to find cookies that don't taste quite as good?

If you can't contribute something that can stand on its own "two feet," it doesn't matter that your competition is lying down on the job. Example: Just because you offer the "best" of all the coffee cup pedestals (little stands to elevate the cup for the sole purpose of avoiding possible coffee rings on one's desk), doesn't mean that a) everyone will buy <u>yours</u>, and b) that it's something anybody needs in the first place. Consider this: if it hasn't been done, maybe it isn't needed. Or, if it hasn't been done, and your dream is calling YOU to do it, then do it before you have ANY competition.

Trade Shows

Trade shows can be valuable sales tools, if they are used constructively and correctly. Trade shows are used to increase sales by effectively displaying your business's products and/or services to potential and existing customers.

Choose your trade shows carefully; only participate in trade shows that your buyers will attend. For some companies, the best shows to attend are national shows that specialize in their industry. For others, smaller regional shows make more sense, as these shows are more convenient and can produce faster results because they are intended to attract the local clientele. Trade show success is measured by reaching the right prospects, otherwise known as "Power Buyers" or "Decision Makers," and concentrating on making sales.

To find out the trade show or convention dates in your city or state, contact the Convention and Visitors

Bureau, or the Chamber of Commerce, and request a complete calendar of shows and events for the year. Early reservations are necessary to ensure a guaranteed booth. The organization in charge of the show or convention will have its own packet of information it will send to you, explaining in detail the schedules, fees, policies, contact people, etc.

Most small businesses cannot afford a national sales force, and many cannot affordably employ a regional staff. Therefore, skillful exhibiting and an organized trade show strategy can produce contacts and sales that normally would be out of reach for the typical business.

Making time count is another important aspect to teach to your trade show team. It can cost between $4,000 and $10,000 per person to create an exhibit and pay wages and overhead. With that kind of investment, results are the objective. To achieve the envisioned results you need from a trade show, we need to focus on the efforts and preparations that put it all together. The usual reasons for exhibiting in a trade show include but are not limited to:

- Introduce your products and/or services to a larger number of prospective customers
- Familiarize potential customers with your products and/or services
- Sell your products and/or services to new customers
- Establish new contacts with distributors, wholesalers, brokers, agents, or others in the marketing and selling industries

- Use the trade show to meet customers you have only spoken to on the phone, and become better acquainted with existing customers
- Shorten the selling cycle with existing customers

Beforehand, meet with your "trade show team" and set goals for sales and contacts. Make sure they are trained, motivated, and enthusiastic about working the show. Inform them that their trade show efforts should be a condensed version of their actual sales pitch that is made in the field, because the serious buyers are trying to obtain as much information as they can, in as little time as they can. However, some buyers attend the shows to discover firsthand or in greater detail products, services, technology, or equipment they are already aware of (including the competition's). Seize the moment and make it work to your advantage.

Use the show time to your fullest advantage by designing an eye-catching display that creates a clear, revealing message stating the benefits and application potential of your products and/or services.

If you're financially able to buy or rent them, use two laptop computers at trade shows; prospects can input their names and addresses into one, and browse through and select information of interest to them in the other. When information of interest is selected, it can then be e-mailed or faxed to their offices. It saves time, money (the cost of preparing brochures and mailing them), and eliminates the extra steps of inputting prospects' information yourself and doing mail-outs. Also, because they have involved themselves in the information-getting process, it is more meaningful to them when they get it.

Merely drawing a large crowd to your booth can be counterproductive, especially if you are giving out free samples. True, the sampling process is vital for consumer identification and acceptance, but what happens is the booth is barraged with sampling or hands-out attendants and the serious buyers will not wait more than a minute for a salesperson's attention. Do not confuse high levels of activity with accomplishment.

When you're dealing with "serious" potential buyers, either close the sale and write the order, or set an appointment time to meet in their place of business or yours. Be sure to run an imprint of their badges, which give you their name and their company's name, address, and telephone number. (Be sure all the information is on the badge; if not, write it on the information sheet your company should have on hand.)

Follow-up on the leads acquired from the show is crucial to trade show success. If an attendee asked for information to be sent, then send it promptly. Customer memory declines in the weeks following a trade show, so it is vital to plan your post-show mailings and sales agenda in advance. As a final note on trade shows—be patient. Some leads will not materialize into sales for months for one reason or another. Communication should not cease because you do not receive an order right away. If you will keep in touch with the "viable" contacts, they will more than likely place their order with your company when the decisions are finalized and the purchase is ready to be made. Check out bookstores for the latest in trade show information and technology.

Mini Bits

Here are a few thoughts to consider when setting up and running your business. Remember, you want to be a successful business. Anyone can throw a business together and hang a sign. If you do it right, you will enjoy a worthwhile pursuit that you can take pride in.

- Compete on value, not price
- Do what you do best
- Grow in your own corner before—or instead of—trying to grow over the block
- Innovate—be daring, different, and delightful!
- If you don't actually want to run the company, find someone who does and will
- Take time to do things right the first time, since you will always have to take the time to do them over
- Quality means never having to say you're sorry; the quality is remembered long after the price is forgotten!

QUESTION: Is putting off procrastination possible?

Gathering Information

Knowing your marketplace requires you to "get educated." This education process requires information and you will need to start gathering it. The more you can get BEFORE you start the business, the better.

One approach to this process is surveys. This class of market research can be do-it-yourself or use those we-do-it-for-you services. In either case:

- Ask what you really want to know
- Ask what you need to know
- Ask what will give you useful information
- Be sure the answers will give you specific "how to be better" information
- Do not double up on information-gathering
- Do not unintentionally ask "useless answer" questions
- Address only one issue per question
- Keep your survey as short as possible, while having it serve your purpose
- Use post-paid postal cards for ease of use in getting the information back to you
- And remember, to get the best answers, ask the best questions

Advertising

I've heard the phrase and used it myself: "You have to advertise to hold on to what you have." In other words, it's used congruously with promotion. Once your business is in motion and the word is out (or you're getting it out) that you're open for business, advertising opens the eyes and ears of your potential customers.

Whether you create your own advertisements or you enlist the service of "professionals," be as creative and alluring as possible. Don't let it be boring. Let's have a little fun with the following advertising samples that have been created for your pleasure. Then create your own attention-getting advertisements with a similar strategy for flair and individuality—for real!

MISS BEA HAVIOR'S FINISHING SCHOOL: FOR THE WOMAN ON HER WAY UP...AND THE LITTLE MAN AT HER SIDE

"THE ONLY PLACE LIKE IT ON EARTH!"

Learn Things That You'll Learn Nowhere Else...

Things Like How to Graciously:

- Butter your bread without a knife
- Retrieve renegade peas to one's plate
- Choose the correct fork with which to scratch your back
- Tip waiters with coupons instead of money
- Deal with a spilled tumbler (or pitcher) of wine
- Cry on que
- Plus many other all-too-little-known niceties

Assisted by Miss N. Form, the woman behind the *Hiding for Health* and *Eating Your Way to Obscurity* best-sellers, Miss B. Havior will make it easy for you to appear correct in any socially ungracious situation. Tuition is only half that of schools that charge twice as much, and your studies require no more time than you would spend doing something else.

To register and begin your training, bring yourself, your inquiring mind, your cashier's check, and a willingness to unlearn the foe poz you've become attached to over a lifetime.

We know being an inept, unaware unsophisticate hurts. Don't suffer through another social catastrophe—call today and learn why several people across America are saying:

"For the answer to life's sticky situations, you can't beat Miss B. Havior with a wooden spoon!"

Call 482-6824 or 462-2563

(I82-MUCH or IMA-CLOD)

GROWTH CENTER REPAIR SHOP

Where our motto is: "If it ain't broken, we can fix that!"

Are you tired of being genuine all the time and standing on your own two feet? Has growing and changing worn you out? Would you like to pass your responsibilities on to someone else for a change?

Well then, come to our 15-minute workshop, where we use the tools we have to set you straight. Our specialists are experts at showing you how to avoid the here and now, with the side benefit to you of learning how to live in the future or the past.

Our system can help you get disorganized and off center, encouraging your outer self to flake or space out once again. **Come To Us—Our Body Shop Promises To Relieve You Of The Burden Of Your Great Potential!** Call IMA PHAKE for reservations, at 222-REAL.

STRESS-FREE LIVING

Tired of losing your keys all the time? Have you tried everything, including regression and the "talking" key chain that was supposed to respond to your voice, but never found a pitch it liked?

We have the answer! Revolutionary KEY-WE, the natural, ultimate answer to a pesky, perennial problem.

We take impressions of all your keys and distribute them to our over 9,000 Key Centers across the country. One is sure to be in a neighborhood near you.

Merely call our 24-hour line, and within minutes, one of our dispatchers will be at your door, a new set of keys in hand.

There is a one-time service charge (less than the cost of two replacement windows, or one car repainting), plus a small yearly maintenance fee (which is lower than the cost of high blood pressure medication).

You've tried everything to remember where you put your keys. Admit it—there's no hope! Let KEY-WE be your key to stress-free living!

CALL MY KEY-WE (695-3993) AND NEVER BE LOCKED OUT AGAIN!

Your Advertising Formula for Success

- Get your customers' attention.
  "Our free samples are BETTER than free. We'll pay you to try them!"

- Hold your customers' attention.
  "We've hidden a miniature of our product inside one out of every 100 boxes we packed this month. If you are the lucky one to find it, bring it in and we'll give you the real thing!"

- Create a desire for your product or service, preferably by appealing to an already-existing need.
  Examples: "Mmmm…smell that aroma!" "Feel that luxurious texture." "Modern design blends your timeless memories into a home for all generations." Everybody needs food, clothing, and shelter; most people need information, transportation, relaxation, motivation, education, stimulation, and beautification. Anything you offer that falls into one of those categories has a pre-existing market, since people already spend money on time. If, however, you choose to offer something that falls outside of these categories— perhaps something you might find in a novelty store—it'll be up to you to find the reason people will want to buy it.

If that's hard to do, you might want to ask yourself why you're behind such a product in the first place!

- Make your offering credible.
  You want it to improve or enhance your customers' lives in some way, but if you make it sound like you should be nominated for sainthood or something more than the Nobel prize for your contribution to mankind, you have that much more to answer for (and that much farther to fall!) when complaints start surfacing that you're not living up to your promises. A simple "Endorsed by the thousands of senior citizens now using our product" works better than "If you use our product, you can look thirty years younger, give up your eyeglasses forever, never need a cane or a wheelchair, and do somersaults with ease."

- Prove its value.
  Use actual photographs; offer free samples and demonstrations; explain how its difference from other similar products or services is at the heart of its value. "While all similar products are good, ours goes one step beyond. Come in and see the difference for yourself. You'll never be satisfied with less again."

- Make it easy to buy or use.

The most wonderful product or service in the world will remain an untapped treasure if you insist on skimping on this aspect of marketing. A better location may double your cost in that area, but triple or quadruple your sales and enable you to stay in business.

- Give reasons for acting NOW.

One-day special; Customer Appreciation Day; TODAY ONLY, prize drawing every hour for those in the store; red-light special; buy one right now, get one free; Friday only: bring in a friend and receive 20 percent off your purchase, 10 percent off your friend's; when our supply is gone, there will be no more!

Advertising Angles

Making your product or service easy to buy or use is as vital to your business success as letting people know that such a thing exists through your advertising efforts. Before you write up your copy, distribute it to your advertising channels, and wait for the sales to roll in, consider this: your copy must reflect you, your product or service, and no one else but you.

Be aware of public happenings.

Read a daily local newspaper; put yourself on the mailing lists for all the cultural, sports, senior citizens, or other local events (as relevant to your business) that are listed in seasonal brochures; or check your town's master calendar at your local chamber of commerce. Keep your eyes and ears open around town: notices on bulletin boards, billboards, utility poles, and what you overhear while in line at the grocery store, in elevators, at the movie theater, at the beauty shop, or at the bakery.

Attach yourself and your product or service to publicized events.

Examples: Your town is having a hot-air balloon day festival. You sell "Don't Let Your Dream Get Away" night lights, softly glowing hot-air balloons "tethered" to the "ground." You set up a little booth in the park, along with the refreshments stand, balloons-on-a-string clown, and other vendors. Or, you park your Femme-mobile outside the hotel where "Women Who Spend Most of Their Time in Their Cars" are having their yearly convention. Could you have a more perfect ready-made market and marketing possibilities?

Have press releases made up.

Did you really think that someone out there would stop what he's doing and create a lovely press release just for you, at the very moment you need it? And then put it in his paper, free of charge, so you can have free publicity without lifting a finger? Well, yes, such a thing does exist somewhere, but not on this planet, so you better not count on it, since it may never happen to you. Prepare your own, and say what you want to have said about you and your business. It may not show up in print exactly as you worded it—editors have their own needs, requirements, standards, and space considerations—but they will be more likely to use your press releases if you appreciate them, thank them, and keep your criticism of the paper, their style, or their editing to yourself. And, of course, they cannot use your press releases at all if they do not have them. (Once one of your press releases shows up in print, you can then clip it and include it with your next press release handouts. Always include your business card with such notices.)

Know the names of the media people you'll be dealing with, and update them every three to six months. Immediately note any changes in your telephone and address file. Ask for them by name when calling. Mention that you liked the way your ad looked, or that you appreciated the good placement they gave your ad, or that the voice used (in TV or especially radio advertising) really conveyed your message in the right spirit.

Always be honest and up-front about your advertising budget. Ask for the best possibilities they can offer within that range. And be sure to let your advertising people sample or experience what it is you do or sell, so that they can put their genuine spirit of liking, loving, and appreciating your product or service behind what they say.

Create your own event.

Give lectures, interviews, demonstrations; give out some of your product for a test study, etc. Offer to teach what you know to specific groups (such as senior citizens, anyone who lives in a particular housing area, women who would love to own Femme-mobiles, etc.). Join someone else for a joint venture. That "someone" may appreciate your help, and you can both profit from it. Write it up in your press release; send it to all the appropriate publications in your area with a brief handwritten note addressed to the media person by name. Be sure you give as much lead time as possible. Offer to write a column now and then, or ongoing, on a subject that reflects your expertise. Do not ask to be paid for this. Volunteer your time, your goods, or your money to worthy causes.

Affiliate yourself with places where would-be buyers mingle.

Join a club, attend meetings; attend rallies, ceremonies, or gatherings for people with dreams—high school job fairs, downtown fairs (check on vendor permits where required if sales—not just networking—will take place), senior citizens' centers, etc. Make friends with the owners of other small businesses in the area and see if they would display your brochures, business cards, or flyers. You could return the favor by sharing information on their business, if relevant, with your customers.

Look for "free listings."

Many publications offer them. Local magazines and newspapers list events (some have special calendars for such listings), showcase new businesses, profile entrepreneurs, accept "fillers" such as interesting photos or tidbits (featuring yourself, your company, your product or service, of course), etc. Some radio and TV stations feature new businesspeople on their early-hour shows. And don't forget about your local university stations.

Offer yourself as a "source of information" to the various media. Example: "If you ever need someone to demonstrate how to safely rewire a lamp for your 'Electricity Is Your Friend' segment on the six o'clock news, feel free to call on me." Or, "Because of the research I had to do in order to perfect my Femme-mobile, I'm a storehouse of information on car parts, electrical systems, aerodynamic design, ten-cylinder motors, and anything to do with the making of cars. Keep my number in your file for future reference."

Sell the Sizzle, Not the Steak

Even though the Femme-mobile has everything a woman could ever want in a car, and it's all top quality, there's no substitute for the way she <u>feels</u> when she's behind the wheel—knowing that every part of her automobile has been lovingly made by women just like her, just for her; women who understand her needs; women who share in the victory drive; women who recognize the achievement of the design and acknowledge her good taste and good fortune. She feels secure, safe, pampered, special, on top of the world. She's a woman on the go, on the way up, and people can see her mark of success. She's today's woman, and her Femme-mobile is taking her places she's never been,

Your Media People and You

Publicity. You need it, they offer it. It's a service and it's "for sale." That makes you the customer, the buyer. Don't be too shy to ask a media sales rep to come to your place of business to give you a presentation of the ad styles, sizes, and prices available.

- Ask if there are any specials right now, or if there is a discount for new advertisers.
- Ask what the terms of payment are, and what recourse you will have if the ad is not correct, unsatisfactory in quality, smaller than stated, or presents some other source of dissatisfaction.
- Ask if they accept camera-ready copy only, or if you can just sketch it out and have them build the ad for you.
- Ask how much more it will cost if they create it.
- Ask if there is a discount for running the same ad several times.
- Ask for the exact size of the ad, and ask to see samples of that size ad. Be sure to measure the samples in front of the sales rep to avoid discrepancies later.
- Ask if you can see the ad before it goes to press.
- Ask if there is an extra charge for placement.
- Ask what other kinds of ads will be on the same page with your ad.
- If a new publication appeals to you, talk with the editor and publisher. Suggest taking an ad in the first issue for half of what would normally be charged. And pay for it half up-front and half after the issue comes out.

Great Expectations, Mediocre Results

We can assume you would not buy a car without knowing anything about it. Would you buy a dress without knowing the price? Would you buy it without knowing if it fit you or was flattering to your figure? There are no blanket guarantees in life, and we all know that just because parts of a car are under warranty, it doesn't mean that you'll never have a problem.

Don't expect bigger miracles from a simple little ad. Your media people will do what they can and what they agreed to do, but they cannot magically make customers flock to you. If one kind of ad doesn't work, try another, or try another medium. If all else "fails," maybe you need some professional advice.

Ad Scams

Do not agree to advertise to faceless voices over the phone. Invite them over, look at their medium, and check their references or endorsements. If they can't wait one more day to accept your advertising, you'd better not accept them. When in doubt, DON'T—cheap prices might be just wasted money. If new publications appeal to you, chat with the editor and publisher. Ask about copy/design/their philosophy.

Cost-Nothing Ways to Advertise

- Word of mouth. You tell. Your customers tell each other.
- You are involved in someone else's promotional campaign. They advertise: "C'mon down! You'll find us right next door to Dinah's Diner."

Or, "We can paint your <u>other</u> car to match any Femme-mobile!"

- You're involved in a newsworthy story that's covered locally, regionally, or even nationally.

- Your product, logo, or some other identifying feature is noticed in the background of a news photo, a piece of videotape edited for a commercial or news show, or a movie.

- You happen to be friends with a celebrity, who happens to be caught on film while in your company, and the media needs to identify you for the photo.

- You invite celebrities (they could be local politicians, if you don't happen to get any response from "real" celebrities) to your place of business during your "open house" or "grand opening" ceremonies. When they show up, make sure to have yourself photographed with them, and see that a copy of the photo gets to all the local papers, along with a bit of copy.

- You keep a large attention-getting poster in your storefront window. Chances are, people will be drawn to it even if they didn't happen to notice your business.

CHAPTER SIX

LEGAL, PATENTS, FINANCIAL, AND THE BUSINESS PLAN

> *Resolve to be honest in all events: And if in your judgment you cannot be an honest lawyer, resolve to be honest without being a lawyer. Choose some other occupation.*
> -Abraham Lincoln, notes for a lecture, 1850
>
> *The first thing we do, let's kill all the lawyers.*
> -Shakespeare, Henry the Sixth, Part VI

Legally On Guard

If you believe you'll succeed as long as you work hard enough, you need to be told—and believe—THAT IS A BIG MYTH. Of course hard work is involved, but you must learn how to skillfully avoid the legal entrapments that can cripple or even devastate you before you ever get going.

I wish small business owners only had to dream about—not experience—the horrors of legal nightmares. Such monsters that may disturb one's sleep are far more preferable to those that daily attack one's business, one's family, or one's very being. Waking up can dismiss the former; going to sleep doesn't do a thing to dismiss the latter.

Lawsuits can destroy the most compelling business strategies in existence. Law books are full of examples of businesses that have gone under from legally induced financial disaster and ruin. Don't become another textbook case. Read, ask questions, consult with experts in the field, and never grow complacent. Don't be afraid to appear ignorant. Consider Ernest Hemingway's words: "Nobody knew anything about it, although they all spoke with great positiveness and strategical knowledge." Ask questions about anything and everything that concerns your business affairs. Consider also the words of the Mad Hatter: "I'm late, I'm late, for a very important date," and never conduct important business in that state of mind.

Also remember: Second opinions, like orange juice, are not just for breakfast anymore!

Legal Abuse Syndrome

Lawyers, questions, depositions, interrogatories, inquisitions; fees, extra fees, more fees, unexpected fees; bills, badgering, bills and more bills; being ignored, misinformed, given mixed messages, patronized, and victimized = SICKNESS = Legal Abuse Syndrome.

We must become familiar with the territory we intend to explore before we set out on our expedition, or our marvelous adventure could well turn into a nightmarish misadventure.

We must really and truly understand the traps, the snares, the "land mines," and every other conceivable source of danger and harm lurking beneath, behind, around, or on the luxurious and otherwise innocent-looking landscape of the business world.

Some of that suffering, in regard to the world of business, can be warded off in advance by following the old adage of "Get it in writing."

When you need a lawyer, select one carefully. It is important to have a lawyer who is patient, willing to explain things you do not understand, knowledgeable and skillful, and lighthearted. Legal matters are stressful!

It is during the initial meeting when you will ask your lawyer to be up-front with you, to put all his cards on the table. There are several considerations to ponder, no matter how much you'd just like to use the one your best friend did. Remember, there is no such adage that states "One lawyer fits all."

Living with Your Lawyer

We live in litigious times. Apparently, we've made suing for what we want as common as working for what we want—and as acceptable, in some circles. When all else fails, and we have something coming to us that we just can't get any other way, we appreciate having the option and opportunity that allows us to take our grievances to court and attempt to protect our rights when they are violated.

To go through a legal activity for a worthwhile cause may be a necessary evil. To go through it because you feel the need to pull someone down just to make yourself stand taller cuts your character and reputation short. Although it is attempted all the time, honor cannot be litigated. Truth cannot be litigated. Pride cannot be litigated. If something is not a matter of money, and a great deal of money (remember to subtract all projected court costs, legal fees, and other expenses, such as profits lost due to time away from work), why subject yourself to the time-draining, energy-draining, emotion-draining, and dignity-draining experience of taking it to the courts? Those who do not know you have no interest in your cause; those who do know you probably know the truth without your having to prove anything in front of a judge or jury. (Of course, if someone takes YOU to court, that is another matter; however, the aforementioned principles all still apply.)

Imagine what our court system would be like if everyone involved had to live by the simplest code of ethics—Is it true? Is it necessary? Is it the right thing to do?—before they could ask questions or introduce facts. Better yet, imagine how much easier business would be if others did not seek to cheat or hurt us.

Finding the Right Lawyer

Conscience and law never go together.
-William Congreve, *The Double Dealer*

A verbal contract isn't worth the paper it's printed on.
-Attributed to Samuel Goldwyn

- If interested in learning a little something about your would-be lawyer (such as where and when he graduated from law school) before you call for your appointment, consult the Martindale-Hubbell legal directory, found in both public and legal libraries (www.martindale. com).

- While on the phone making the appointment, ask if you will be charged for the initial consultation, how much time is normally allocated for that visit, and what you should bring to that meeting.
- In the meeting, ask if a situation such as yours can be handled without hiring a lawyer.
- Ask if the lawyer feels positive about your case, believes you are in the right, and is willing to see it through. Honesty up-front can redirect your focus to avoid unnecessary and unrewarding legal steps.
- Be aware of how you feel when you first meet the lawyer. Is there an instinctive like or dislike?
- Notice the language used with you. Is it clear, understandable, and precise?
- How are phone calls handled, or other interruptions? Someday, you may be an interruption.
- Check on fees early in the interview. Ask what the hourly charges are. If

working on a contingency basis, ask what is taken out for expenses.

- Ask if an up-front retainer is required before any work is begun, and the amount.
- Ask if your bill will be itemized (you want it to be) to help you understand exactly what you are paying for.
- Ask what happens if there is a discrepancy over the fees, and if you will be charged for the time it takes to resolve the matter.
- Ask for the bottom-line figure that your case could cost.
- Find out what kind of approach is preferred: peaceful resolution, or go for the throat.
- Ask how much experience in matters like yours the firm has had, and how much of the work she will handle herself.
- Ask how long the law firm has been in business.
- Ask if information can be obtained from the secretary or assistant when the need arises.
- Ask if it is a priority of the firm to return calls on a daily basis, so you will not have to wait too long for answers.
- Ask what time frame you can expect before your case is started on.

- Ask how long your case can be expected to take.
- Ask about the possible outcomes.
- Ask how often you'll be informed of your case's progress, and in what manner.
- Ask if anyone else will be working on the case, who it will be, and ask to meet him or her.
- Ask if mediation and mandatory arbitration might be a possibility for your case, and what her expert opinion is regarding these for your situation.
- Ask if you'll receive copies of all pertinent documents, and what you'll be charged per page.
- Ask if you can have a glass of water, a cup of coffee, some cookies… anything!

Above all, don't be shy. Your lawyer will not be shy about billing you for services rendered.

Once you have made your decision to hire a particular lawyer, ask for the details of your understanding to be put in writing, including all fees, estimates of any additional costs, as well as what the retainer will be. This fee should then be placed into a trust account that is only used to pay for expenses related to your legal case. Once it is depleted, you will probably be required to put more money into the account. In essence, you are paying up-front. What is not billed out is refunded to you. Ask to make sure.

Legal Briefs

It's not what you spend, it's what you get for your money. If a lawyer charges "only" $250 an hour, is she a better buy for your money than a lawyer who charges three times as much? Not if the "cheaper" lawyer takes five times as long to get the job done. Those "per hour" fees add up fast.

You can get a copy of your state's bar association Code of Professional Conduct from a library or the bar association itself. You can and should report your lawyer to the appropriate disciplinary agency in your state if you believe there has been a breach of ethics. In most states, complaint hearings against attorneys are open to the public. (Ask about the bar association's free dispute-free resolution program.)

Most states have a client-protection fund available to those who can prove their lawyer is in possession of unearned legal fees. You must file a claim, appear before a voluntary panel of attorneys, and prove dishonesty or misconduct on the part of your attorney.

PLEASE NOTE: In spite of it all, remember: lawyers did not create the problems that led you to their offices. Do not take out your indignation over your predicament on them. When they act with integrity—and we will assume this until and unless we have reason to believe otherwise—you will be grateful for their professional help.

The Law Will Out

How amazing it is that, in the midst of controversies on every conceivable subject, one expects unanimity of opinion upon difficult legal questions! In the highest ranges of thought, such as theology, philosophy, and science, we find differences of view on the part of the most distinguished experts—theologians, philosophers, and scientists. The history of scholarship is a record of disagreements!

An Ounce of Prevention Is Worth a Pound of Cure

No one could have said it better than Benjamin Franklin! The only thing better than getting out of litigation is staying out of it. To possibly avoid legal entanglements, include the "ADR" (Alternative Dispute Resolution) technique clause in EVERY contract you sign. This is a possible settlement approach through arbitration or mediation which brings the defendants and their lawyers together for a day with both sides stating their case. This approach basically enables you to settle a dispute during the infant stages of litigation rather than dragging you through the courts. This would save you thousands of lost dollars and hundreds of lost hours. Some community colleges offer classes in Alternative Dispute Resolution techniques. Nonetheless, consult with your legal counsel about it.

Be smart about retaining a lawyer. If you do not feel comfortable with a particular lawyer, the relationship will not get any better. If a lawyer has a problem realizing you are a customer, chances are there will be other problems that arise.

> *The law is not a brooding omnipresence in the sky.*
>
> -O.W. Holmes

A Return to Common Sense

We seem to have forgotten two indispensable ingredients of any successful human endeavor. The first is use of judgment. We have constructed a system of regulatory law that basically outlaws common sense. Modern law, in an effort to be "self-executing," has shut out our humanity. And as the process has developed into a kind of religion, we have forgotten about the second ingredient—responsibility.

courtroom dramas do not touch most of our lives but the law of government, on the other hand, controls almost every activity of common interest—fixing the pothole in front of the house, running public schools, regulating day-care centers, supervising the workplace, cleaning up the environment and regulating interest rates.

Amazing how we Americans can do almost anything. We will figure it out, and if we don't, we will work so hard that it won't matter. Our energy has always amazed foreigners. As the nineteenth-century French observer Alexis de Tocqueville wrote: "No sooner do you set foot on American soil than you find yourself in a sort of tumult; a confused clamor rises on every side and a thousand voices are heard at once...All around you, everything is on the move."

Whenever the rules are eased, our energy and good sense pour in like sunlight through opened blinds. After the 1994 earthquake in Los Angeles toppled freeways, California Governor Pete Wilson suspended the thick book of procedural guidelines and, using federal aid, authorized financial incentives for speedy work. Instead of a four-year trudge through the government process, the Santa Monica Freeway was rebuilt in sixty-six days, to a higher standard than the old one.

From the law's perspective, the Los Angeles repair project was a nightmare of potential abuse. The process wasn't completely objective; almost nothing was spelled out to the last detail. When the rule book was tossed, all that was left was judgment and responsibility. State officials decided which contractors would be allowed to bid, and they knew they would be accountable if the contractors proved unreliable. Instead of specifying every iron rod, state inspectors took responsibility for checking to make sure that the work complied with general standards. When disagreements occurred, the contractor and the state bureaucrats worked them out, just as if they were real people. And they got it done in record time.

The sunlight of common sense shines high above us whenever principles control what is right and reasonable, and do not allow the parsing of legal language to ubiquitously dominate the discussion. With this goal shining always before us, the need for lawyers fades, along with the receding legal shadows. We have a fundamental desire to understand what is expected of us. We should be able to redevelop the attributes we used to value most: effort, courage, and leadership.

As Tocqueville put it, having "the chance to make mistakes that can be retrieved" is the "great privilege" of Americans. More than anything else, it is what defined the American spirit. So, when we wake up every morning, we have to go out and try to accomplish our goals and resolve disagreements by doing what we think is right and reasonable. Our energy, resourcefulness, judgment, and responsibility, not millions of legal restrictions, are what is great about us, and about our country. There is nothing unusual or frightening about this. Relying on ourselves is not, after all, a new ideology. It is just common sense!

Virtual Legal Help

Wouldn't you know it, in this day and age, that we would be able to turn to the Internet once again for some sound legal guidance and help? If you need some basic legal questions answered, go to www.justanswer.com and select your area of questioning from the drop-down menu. Another avenue to research, www.legalmatch. com, is a free and confidential service to consumers that matches attorneys to clients per case. You simply state your case and interested local (or out of state, depending on circumstance) lawyers respond. You are able to privately review the pricing details, attorney profiles, ratings by previous users, and specific information about your case and then you choose the attorney that's best for you.

For ease of use and savings of time you can find legal forms at www.myeasyforms.com. They have an array of legal forms like by-laws, meeting minutes, power of attorney, and everything else you could possibly use in your daily business dealings.

The Institute for Professional and Executive Development, Inc., www.ipedinc.net, a Washington, D.C.-based seminar company for wage and hour litigation, offers help to professionals with education-based seminars on the most current industry practices in today's ever-changing competitive and regulatory environments.

Another service offered is a contract workforce administration that will handle your contractors' payments for you, as well as their W-2s and 1099s. Using contractors can be complex and intimidating, so they offer customized solutions and pricing proposals that help to keep you efficient, profitable, and focused on what you do best. Log onto www.mybizoffice.gov (actually listed under mybizofficeMBO) for more information and research (and there's a lot of it).

Patents, Trademarks, and Registrations

Put your talent in your work and your genius in your life.
                                    -Oscar Wilde

Private property is a natural fruit of labor.
                                    -Pope Pius XII

Protecting Your Property—You Made It, You Need to Patent It

A patent is a grant by the United States Patent and Trademark Office which gives the patent owner (the inventor or the assignee, which could be you) the right to exclude others from making, using, and selling the invention protected by the patent.

Patents are categorized into three basic types: utility, design, and plant (biological). A patent may be obtained for a new, useful, and non-obvious process, machine, manufacture, or composition of matter. Most applications claim inventions of one of these types.

Basic Steps for Getting Your Patent

Whatever it is you wish to patent must meet either the non-obvious or the novelty requirements. Information on patents is subject to change. Always update your information before proceeding. Patent attorneys who specialize in this field can give you the latest information, and they can professionally handle all correspondence associated with properly guiding your project through the maze of patent application puzzlement and paper.

Novelty Search

Patentability most often hinges upon the non-obvious requirement rather than upon the requirement of novelty. The purpose of a novelty search is to research and find out if there are prior patents on similar inventions. The searches are typically conducted in the Patent Office by professional searchers retained by the patent attorney. The search might also be conducted outside the Patent Office through databases, product literature, or some other technical source. If other patents similar to yours exist, the quest is over, unless yours can be altered or its uniqueness can be argued and proved (which is usually too expensive to pursue, on the premise that you could lose the argument thousands of legal dollars later).

The cost of a novelty search is based on the amount of time spent searching, plus the hourly rate of the searcher. Your attorney will then review this search and make a recommendation to you as to whether or not an application should be filed, and the scope of the anticipated patent protection.

If the invention appears patentable, the patent attorney will prepare and file a patent application that describes, defines, and carefully claims the invention so that the broadest and most obtainable patent may be sought. Your patent attorney will coordinate the entire process and include patent drawings carefully prepared by a patent draftsman. The time it takes will depend upon the completeness of the information you provide, the complexity of the invention, the number of revisions required, and the number of times you must meet with your attorney before the final draft is made and the application is sent.

The U.S. Patent and Trademark offices require fees for the filing of a patent application, and the issuance and then maintenance of the actual patent. For small entities, including individual inventors and companies employing fewer than 500 employees, special rates apply.

EXAMPLES:

Basic utility application fee	$315
Design fee	$125
Plant fee	$210
Utility issue fee	$525
Design issue fee	$185
Plant issue fee	$260

For large entities, the fees are doubled. There are numerous other fees, such as for extensions of time to respond, petition fees, appeal fees, and late payment fees, most of which are basic.

What Comes Next

The Patent and Trademark Office will then examine the application to see if it meets the requirements for novelty and non-obviousness, and its other formal requirements. There are a number of possible outcomes. A patent will only be granted if the patent office concludes that ALL requirements have been met. Contact the U.S. Commissioner of Patents and Trademarks and request information regarding the application and granting process for patents, trademarks, and registrations (U.S. Commissioner of Patents and Trademarks, Washington, DC 20231; 703-308-HELP; www.uspto.gov).

Seeking a patent requires patience. Due to the backlog of patents pending and of the particular operating group (within the patent office) to which your application is assigned, you can expect it to take up to two years or so to obtain a patent, after date of filing.

Advantages

Obtaining a patent gives you the right to exclude others from making, using, or selling your invention in the United States for a period of seventeen years.

Trademarks

A trademark is a "word" (name, symbol, logo, etc.) which is created for and used by a company to identify its products and to distinguish them from other products sold by competing companies.

When selecting a trademark, it is important to select a word which you can prevent competitors from using for the same or very similar products or services. From a legal point of view, distinctive terms are preferable to suggestive terms; both are preferred over descriptive terms. Generic terms cannot function as trademarks.

After selecting a trademark, and prior to using it, consult with your attorney about conducting a comprehensive search to determine if there are any prior uses, registered or unregistered, that possibly could affect the use of your selected trademark.

A filing fee of at least $210 (at this writing) must accompany the written trademark application. Trademarks registered with the federal government are valid for ten years and may be renewed if the goods and/ or services are still in interstate use.

Copyrights

Copyright protects "original works of authorship." This includes a broad spectrum of works, and you should consult with an attorney familiar with copyright law to obtain explanations of the details involved with copyrights. Contact the Library of Congress to request such information or to file for an application for registration of your copyright (Library of Congress, Copyright Office, 101 Independence Ave. SE, Washington, DC 20557; 202-707-3000).

A $20.00 filing fee (at this writing) must accompany each copyright application. Copyrights exist for the life of the author and an additional fifty years after the author's death, or a total of seventy-five years for an organization.

Financing, Banking, and Other Sources

> *I have all the money I'll ever need if I die by 4 o'clock.*
>
> -Henry Youngman

Some Creative Financing Sources

As dedicated entrepreneurs, we may find ourselves in situations that require going beyond the normal or traditional methods of obtaining money. The financial techniques provided here are certainly not the only nontraditional avenues available. As long as the human brain is able to function, there will continue to be newer, more flexible, creative, and artistic capital-raising ideas brought to light. That is exciting in itself!

The main goal is to help you understand what your options are, how to explore them, what avenues to research, and even what people or companies to contact for assistance. You are never at a dead end—only a detour—if the way you've chosen doesn't work out for you. Discover the range of possibilities and let your imagination take over. There are no boundaries for creative financing; the only limitations are the hours in a day. Preparation is the key.

Creative financing-related books worth checking out:

1. *Guerrilla Financing: Alternative Techniques to Finance Any Small Business*, by Bruce Blechman and Jay Conrad Levinson (Houghton Mifflin, 1991). $10.95.
2. *Money Sources For Small Business*, by William Alarid (Puma Publishing, Santa Maria, California, 800-255-5730, ext. 110). A 224-page listing of venture capital groups, plus some state and local investment programs which are available. $19.95.

You might enjoy engaging yourself in some one-on-one contact with the following sources for some up-front guidance and assistance:

1. AWED—American Women's Economic Development Corp., 800-222-AWED. They offer courses on management, training, and business counseling, plus they sponsor an annual conference in New York City for women in business, and those dreaming of starting a business.
2. Women's World Banking, 8 West Fortieth Street, 10th Floor, New York, NY 10018; 212-768-8513. They have more than a thousand affiliates worldwide, ranging from bankers to lawyers, government people to business people, all committed to helping women.

3. NASBIC (National Association of Small Business Investment Companies). Contact to request their booklet "Venture Capital—Where to find it" (NASBIC, P.O. Box 2039, Merrifield, VA 22116; 202-628-5055). Cost is $20. Ask for a list of their other publications on small business financing while you're at it.

Venture Capital Drawbacks

These items could keep a venture capitalist from investing in your company:

- Easy competition
- Few salable assets
- Built-in obsolescence
- Advantages not apparent enough
- Too avant-garde
- Too limited in scope
- New waters—no experience

There is nothing etched in stone as a guide for approaching lenders and investors; no chartered course to follow, only guidelines and sound advice. New players come into the picture every year, both on the lending side as well as the borrowing side. Take your best-laid-out plans incorporated into a request for financing to the lending source and let them determine the merits and weigh the risks involved.

The "experts" will compare your information with their own data and knowledge and either provide the funding or give you a rejection. If you have a caring lending source, it might give you positive feedback to help you fine-tune and ultimately receive the funds. Don't give up if one door closes, somewhere else a window will open! If you truly believe in your dream and its success, keep on trying. Here are a few more possibilities for you to explore.

Personal Savings

There is no question that funding a start-up will require the investment of your personal savings such as money, savings accounts, bonds, stocks, and retirement plans. The advantage to financing a business this way is that you can run your business the way you want because it is your money. The disadvantage is that you can lose as much money as you invest.

Credit Cards

Many successful entrepreneurs have used their credit cards for start-up capital or an injection of quick money when they were at a critical point in cash requirements. I can remember back to some early business days of being so "creditworthy" that I had in my possession eight gold credit cards and maxed out the limits to a total of $35,000. For the onlookers only, my title was the "Queen of Credit." Others thought it was impressive to have ALL those cards. To me, it meant survival for a growing company. It was hell to pay back with the high interest rates, but those credit cards were a source when the banks tightened their lending or developed attitudes of control I didn't like. There are plenty of success stories out there about this type of self-financing. The advantages include drawing up to 80 percent cash value of your credit limit without going through a time-consuming process of paperwork, updated financial statements, or dealing with people and explaining why you need the money.

The disadvantages include exhausting your credit limit and paying an enormous interest rate, which is usually higher than traditional lending institution rates. This should be a last resort type of self-financing because the payback can be tough!

Friends and Relatives

Borrowing from those you know and can convince that you have a workable plan is probably your next best source of financing. You will have more success with this type of financing if you come up with a monthly repayment plan, complete with a due date and a fair interest rate. The advantage to borrowing from these sources is that the money can be obtained quicker and usually is accompanied by a more reasonable rate of interest than traditional sources.

The disadvantage is often the "too-close-for-comfort" phrase, unless everything is discussed and agreed upon beforehand by both sides, with a legal document drawn up outlining the loan and repayment procedures.

Banks and Credit Unions

You must prove to these sources that you do not really need the money! Just kidding—well, sort of. (Checking to see if you're still with me.)

You must prove that you are a creditworthy customer. Even then it is difficult to obtain funding. Often, the loan can take months to finalize before actual funding occurs, attached to miscellaneous fees such as filing fees, appraisals, commitment fee points, and legal expense.

Bankers want to know:

- The borrower's track record
- How they will be repaid

The loans banks make to businesses are almost always heavily collateralized by homes and other personal assets. It is very rare for a bank to make a loan to any company less than three years of age. So, with this in mind, and if you qualify to approach a bank, you may as well gather together information they will definitely request before they proceed any further with your proposal. This includes:

- A current balance sheet
- A profit and loss statement
- A current list of assets
- A cash flow statement
- Names of your key suppliers and customers
- Information on insurance coverage (business and personal) and a succession plan

If you feel you need help in preparing for a bank loan, a workbook has been created by Robert Morris Associates (RMA) of Philadelphia, Pennsylvania, called "Business Credit Information Package." Within the thirty-page workbook are basic forms for you to complete that will supply lenders with the information they will surely ask for. The workbook provides worksheets for compiling simplified balance sheets, profit and loss statements, and cash flow statements. Order the workbook by contacting RMA at 800-766-7621. The cost is $13.00 at this writing. They also have a catalog listing of other items available you may request.

A bank-related book worth reading:

> *Borrowing For Your Business*, by George M. Dawson (Upstart Publishing, Dover, NH; 800-235-8866). A former banker explains how bankers evaluate small companies. $16.95.

If the loan gets turned down, don't just sit around licking your wounds and blaming the banker for not seeing your venture in the same light as you do. You are in the company of thousands of others who were turned down, but turned it around. Use the opportunity to round up the reasons why the banker said no. Ask for advice to learn if the bank sees a credit weakness in your company or a weakness in your presentation. The idea is to get everything out of the banker that you can, to help you figure out where you're "missing it." There is no banking "ethics rule" that will assure you the banker is being totally up-front and helpful to you, but if you will be diplomatic in your request, the chances of you getting those answers will be very good. Now, on to the next avenue of creative financing sources.

Loan Pools

This is a hybrid of sorts between traditional bank financing and venture capitalist funding. A pool usually consists of a group of local individuals who lend their pooled money to companies in a specific industry. Begin with your banker, accountant, or a finance consultant to find out if they know of such pools in existence that would apply to your needs.

Common Stock

Issuing company stock is a method of raising substantial amounts of capital. Do keep in mind, however, that you are essentially selling partial ownership rights of your company in the process. Common stockholders enjoy certain rights, such as:

- Control of the company. Stockholders elect the company's board of directors, who in turn elect top management. If you remain the majority stockholder, you or the person you appoint may assume the president and chairman of the board positions.
- Preemptive right, which is the right to purchase any new stock your company issues. Check with your state and your "corporate charter" for the details.

Bonds

Issuing bonds is another method of long-term financing for corporations. There are several types of corporate bonds. Check with your CPA to guide you in these areas:

- Trust Bonds—secured by a specific piece of equipment
- Collateral Trust Bonds—secured by anything that is not real estate
- Convertible Bonds—can be exchanged for a certain number of shares of common stock

Factoring

For businesses that sell on terms and need the cash before the accounts receivables come in, factoring may be something for you to explore. Factoring is an alternative to traditional methods of financing because these companies specialize in lending against invoices, and the burden of worthiness is based on your customers' credit, not on yours. Factoring companies charge a percentage of the amount funded as their commission fee, which can range anywhere from 3 percent to 8 percent of the gross pledged amount, along with any administrative costs and fees.

Be sure to examine each factoring company closely because they differ from one to the next. Shop and compare before deciding, and check references. For more information regarding factoring sources, consult your local bankers, accountants, business periodicals (advertisements), or industry groups.

Angels

Otherwise known as an individual investor (usually with a high net worth), who is willing to provide money and support to a start-up or expanding company in exchange for an equity interest. These are usually looking for a big return on investments made in early-stage companies, and some are even prepared to write off an investment as a total loss.

There are now more than 200 angel organizations—up from only ten in 1996. Angels frequently are entrepreneurs who have done well and want to help others do well. They still want to make money. As a rule, an investor of any type must be confident in the management of a company and interested in the type of industry the company functions in. Finding people who know your industry is the best thing to do, but is not always possible. Therefore, the weight of convincing a potential investor is shifted to your business plan, along with the experience and abilities of the management team. You WILL need to have a very well-structured business plan ready when seeking angel investments.

To find angel investors in your area, contact the Angel Capital Education Foundation, c/o Kauffman Foundation, 4801 Rockhill Rd., Kansas City, Missouri 64110 (www.angelcapitaleducation.org).

Franchising

The idea behind franchising a company is to duplicate your business and grow with it nationally, with the team effort of aggressive and energized people who want to own their own business. It is an expensive venture both for the franchisor and the franchisee.

The hardest part of the venture is to find people who meet the minimum financial requirements in net worth and are willing to pay a hefty franchise fee, plus royalty fees and advertising fees, and possibly rental fees for the land and building, etc., but plenty of them are out there.

For a substantial listing of franchisors, search www. franchiscompanies.com or www.thefranchisecompany. com.

The Business Plan

> *"The credit belongs to the man who is actually in the arena, whose face is marred by dust and sweat and blood; who strives valiantly; who errs and comes short again and again, who knows the great enthusiasms, the great devotions, and spends himself in a worthy cause; who at the best, knows the triumph of high achievement; and who, at the worst, if he fails, at least fails while daring greatly, so that his place shall never be with those cold and timid souls who know neither victory nor defeat."*
>
> -Theodore Roosevelt

The business plan is both a map and an itinerary. It provides help in plotting the course of direction and time frames for such things as projections or forecasting financial conditions. The business plan should encompass as much information pertinent to your business as you can gather that will give you valuable assistance in plotting the course of direction for your destination.

The main reason for putting together a business plan is so that you can use the data to build, grow, and manage the company. Its contributions will help management in areas such as company goals, the mission statement, structure, direction, borrowing money from a bank, selling company stock, financial information, analysis of markets and trends, projections, competition—you name it, and it should be there.

The objective is to be concise, articulate, and to the point, while underscoring the fact that management has done their homework and knows the business as well as the market they are in.

If you are in an existing business and do not have a prepared business plan, now is the perfect time to prepare one, using the following guide. Doing the research at your city college or university business school library makes the task easier, because you can enlist the help of the very knowledgeable assistants and librarians who will save you time by giving specific directions to your requests. When you are finished, create a nice cover and have the manual spiral bound at a local quick printing store, and then put it to use, expecting great things to be accomplished as planned.

The Nuts and Bolts of the Business Plan

The business plan is a set of blueprints your company will use to build and grow by. You will need to revise and update it occasionally so it remains current in overall knowledge of your business operations.

If you feel that you need more helping hands in creating your company's business plan, there are exceptionally well-written guidelines and computer programs in bookstores, computer stores, and SBA offices that offer inexpensive help.

With a business plan, you creatively set a course of direction for your company by articulating thoughts and placing them in order of priority, thus developing a definite course of direction. Follow that path, allowing here and there for a shift in pattern changes. As the founder and orchestrator of the company, you will assess potential markets, define product and/or service, and state who is going to operate areas of the business and in what capacity.

We're going to take this in a step-by-step approach to make the task of writing a business plan as simple as possible. But remember the bottom line—it requires your personal knowledge put into words that are going to set the itinerary and course of direction. While there are no rules written in stone for creating the perfect business plan, the outcome will depend greatly on the nature of your business, its history (if it has one), the complexity of the organization, the products, service or technology, the management, plus other personal factors relevant to your business.

A standard business plan should be between twenty-five and fifty pages in length, and be as brief but informative as possible. Let your creative juices flow, creating whatever format you choose, while at the same time incorporating the following contents:

1. EXECUTIVE SUMMARY
   The executive summary should be summarized on one page, if possible, and should state:

- The business name and description
- Product/service description
- Nature of your market
- Management profiled briefly
- Overview of financial projections
- The financial structure and needs

TIP: While this is the first section in your business plan, it should be the last section that you write. After writing the business plan, the compiled information is what you will review and summarize to write the executive summary.

2. BUSINESS DESCRIPTION AND HISTORY

This section will provide the background of the business. The business name should be fully stated, with the date and place of formation, along with other historical accounts such as ownership, legal structure, products, and past and present events that have propelled the business into notoriety or brought special attention. The business plan should also describe any subsidiaries or partners, along with the principals, for their roles of starting the business.

Details should be slightly expounded on here regarding objectives you have developed that will determine whether your business is on track. These objectives should be a representation of your business's activities in terms of measurable targets within the industry standards. Easy to understand and briefly presented, its contents might include:

- Gross Revenues
- Net Income
- Return on Investment
- Market Share and/or Dominance
- Production Progress
- Customer Base Increase

State what the company's goals are relating to these areas, along with the current status of each.

3. PRODUCT OR SERVICE DESCRIPTION
Describe the product or service lines of your business. Explain what sets yours apart from the competition, what makes it unique, and what the competitive advantages are of your product/service over the products/service of your competition. When possible, provide statistics, reviews, or independent product evaluation reports.

If your company is still in the development process, provide the current position of your venture, contrasted with where your schedule for completion will put you once you begin. Be sure to mention if you have any patents or patents pending, trademarks, or copyrights that you own or are in the process of applying for.

If your company is in the process of building any equipment or developing any type of high technology, describe it briefly. Explain what the approximate time frame will be to completion and availability, and how your business plans to make the most of the new developments once they are set in motion or completed. If applicable, explain how these changes will impact new and further product developments.

4. MARKET ANALYSIS AND APPROACH
   Explain how you plan to approach and enter the market initially with your products or services, and what sets you apart from the competition. Explain why your products will be accepted and how you plan on initiating them into action. Explain how your products or services will not only generate a return on investment

or break even, but will also make a profit. This is a very important section in your business plan. You must create a mood of confidence in others, that you understand the market for your product in addition to understanding what it will take to introduce it into the marketplace.

You will need to identify the main markets for the industry, such as consumer, commercial, or government. Research and note from your findings if political, social, or economic changes may negatively or positively impact your product/ service. Explain the growth rate of the markets in comparison to other similar markets.

Identify major targeted customers and their sales history or future contractual commitments. Explain what percentage of your sales volume these customers would and/or do represent. Explain if possible that each major customer may have different purchasing habits or policies, and then explain how you will approach them; i.e., distributors, franchising, outside sales representatives, brokers, telemarketing, or direct mail. If you plan to sell to the end user or consumer, explain the sales cycle completely and the pricing method; i.e., by the unit, case, periodic contract, or through competitive bidding. Include any market surveys you have conducted and describe the results in this section.

Assess any price sensitivities you have discovered through your polling of prospective customers, and if they had any substantial responses to your proposed products or services. If any actual product testing was done, give the results.

Discuss the different aspects associated with your products; for example, are there any external influences that may cause demand to rise and fall, is it a seasonal product or service, or is it steady.

Summarize the strategies you will use for your marketing and public relations efforts. Outline the advertising and promotion plans. If you plan to use outside sources for the marketing effort, state the individuals' or company's names, describe their industry expertise, and if possible give some names of their present and/or past clients or customers.

5. COMPETITION

Your research should bring to light all aspects of the market, including the competitors. Now it is time to describe their strengths and their weaknesses. Discuss their market share as well as how customers perceive them. This is not an opportunity to throw stones at them; keep it professional, with the analysis respectfully in perspective.

6. KEY PERSONNEL

This section is different from your personnel plan, in that here you are individually profiling the principals and key management personnel who will bring special talents to the business. It is not necessary to include resumes, for those can be placed in the appendix. You should expound on the individual experience of each, the level of position each will hold in the business operations, and state if special or extraordinary salary or stock arrangements have been provided.

7. OPERATING PLAN

This is the meat and potatoes section of how your business will operate. This section should inform on topics such as facilities, personnel, manufacturing or the business process, contractors, suppliers, customers, technologies, and skills required to manufacture, process, or deliver the product or service. The total business environment should be portrayed through words that accurately describe day-to-day operations, including the staffing of each area, number of employees employed (or needed), job descriptions of each (if employees are currently a part of your business), with an overall master schedule of when the business will be open and how (if applicable) the shift changes will be structured.

Include your present plan for accomplishing production demands, and how the assembly line will be organized. Explain how you will maintain quality control and monitor efficiency. If you contract out part or all of your production, explain how you will maintain quality and efficiency controls, and what particular arrangements you have made with the contract company. Will the inventory be satisfactory to supply the demands, or do you have several outlets to draw from?

NOTE: This section could become quite lengthy as you unfold the operations of the business. Some companies break down the different aspects of the business into individual sections, and then summarize these into a company plan with an overview.

The detailed information must be available to support your explanations and findings to a potential investor or analyst at a later time. While this section is being researched and written, make certain you have included the related costs. The up-front expenses such as rent, utilities, and general administrative costs are fixed. The variable expenses are those that are tied directly to production expenses or sales expenses.

Consistent monthly recordkeeping will contribute to your financial analysis section. These records will assist you in determining exactly what costs are involved in operating the business and what will be the break-even point.

8. FINANCIAL ANALYSIS
Everything in the business eventually boils down to the bottom line. The business projections, plans, and actual operations are based on what

the bottom line says to do. If the numbers are there, it's easier to go forward. If the numbers are not there, an injection of capital (money) is needed. Seeking adequate financing will become necessary for keeping the company on course.

The existence of your business must be justified to a group of serious, profit-oriented investors. You will be required to predict the financial results of the company projected over a five-year period. That sounds like *Fantasy Island*, being able to project the future, but it is important to attempt to control the events surrounding the business for its survival and growth.

Many businesses meet and exceed their five-year projections. Just be sure and put your all into this section, because it will be the most carefully analyzed section of the business plan. Consult with your CPA and ask for assistance with these projections that are planning your company's future. The investors will want professional books and controls established, so the help from your company's CPA means there will be active involvement on her part to see the company through to success, a direct benefit—keeping a customer as a growing customer!

Once you have obtained the financing you were seeking and the business is operational, refer to the business plan as a working, integral part of the business affairs. Update its contents to keep it current or to allow for shifts in trends, then follow your plans carefully, avoiding the perils of straying off course.

Consult with experts when it comes to writing this business plan, especially if you don't even know what one looks like (the above references ARE a business plan outline, if you care to do it yourself), or if you have trouble writing about ideas and strategies. Remember, the SBA office is available for assistance and they have sample plans for your convenience. They also offer workshops in writing business plans and offer coaching and feedback that is constructive and nonthreatening.

There are university students specializing in writing business plans who can do it for a fraction of the cost of what your CPA would charge you. The MBA programs of university business schools are a great source to begin your search.

These sources of information relative to writing a business plan are available for purchase, if you care to look into them:

- The SBA's business plan outlines, which are industry-specific and cost about a dollar each, are available at your local SBA office or SBDC. The advantage to these industry-specific business plan outlines is that the guidelines for structuring plans can vary substantially from industry to industry; knowing them at the beginning can be a significant advantage to you.

- Multimedia MBA Small Business Edition, published by Compact Publishing, Inc. Richard D. Irwin, publisher of business books for professionals and college students, has prepared a CD-Rom package offering templates and business expertise in preparing business plan templates, accounting tools, human resource templates and forms, legal forms, and many more specialized applications to help any small business with guidance and solutions. Cost is about $89.

CHAPTER SEVEN

EMPLOYEES AND THE EMPLOYEE HANDBOOK

A Little More Than You

One of the most important and critical aspects of running your own business concerns your employees. They must be treated in accordance with federal and state laws, and you must adhere to the proper procedures when dealing with them. It is imperative that you know the local, state, and federal regulations, so do your research. Nothing can cripple your business quicker than an employee's legal suit that catches you in the middle of strong company growth. The whole atmosphere can be changed from an upbeat, happy, stimulating challenge to a quagmire of negativism and legal entanglements, choking off all positive movement and fresh air.

The manager or employee who put you in the position of being sued can stay and continue working and be paid, resign, be fired, or walk away and go work elsewhere. In contrast, the legal and financial responsibility falls on the shoulders of you (the owner) and your company. You are responsible for your employees' actions, whether it is of sexual, religious, or race discrimination, product sabotage, trust type documents altered, breech of contracts, etc. You will be the one who must stay and face the consequences.

If this chapter does nothing more than save you from the gut-wrenching nightmare of a lawsuit, I'll know I did my part well.

It is not possible to educate you in all the areas of employee-related matters—there will always be a "new one on us," people being what they are. But the one thing I do want to get across to you is that you <u>must</u> get smart about such employment practices as those covering equal opportunity, job descriptions, contracts, benefits, personnel, payroll records, taxes, drug and alcohol prescreening, and interviewing. Follow the rules. Keep your records accurate and then LOCK THEM UP!

Gifts of the Heart

Remember, there are a lot of good people in the workforce and they deserve to be treated with respect and dignity. These are the team players that you will hopefully attract for your business's continued growth.

Employees are not to be thought of as your potential "problems." Many of them will be a source of much satisfaction and even joy. Employees can give a lot to their job, their company, and to YOU, as their employer. They can give what amounts to gifts, above and beyond what is required or expected of them. They can give to your business:

Gifts of the Mind

Employees can help your business through their intelligence and experiences by:

- Offering their expertise and their suggestions for improvement, above and beyond their job description.
- Giving their help in solving problems or answering difficult questions.

Gifts of Time and Words

Employees can provide numerous gifts of their time and good words to help make your day or help your business succeed. Employees help the business by:

- Being or making themselves available for additional responsibilities, overtime, extra duties.
- Offering guidance where needed, where appropriate, and when asked.
- Helping out above and beyond what is expected. ("Even though we couldn't have the report ready by five p.m. today, I don't mind working on it for a few hours tonight so it can be ready for your eight a.m. meeting tomorrow.")

A Good Employee Is Hard to Find, and Where to Find Them

There are two kinds of work one can do:
The kind one enjoys and the kind one does best.
If the two are the same, one truly is blessed.

Networking

It is often necessary to network in order to find good folks to work in your business. That network must include all of the normal means, but also may require you to look beyond the local circles. Consider:

- Employment agencies, private and government, and classified ads
- Employment bulletin boards
- Trade schools, community colleges, and other schools
- Community organizations and clubs
- Churches, synagogues, and religious centers
- Veterans organizations and clubs
- Government-sponsored programs
- Referrals from friends and relatives
- Libraries
- Community information centers
- Unsolicited applicants who show up when you need them
- Internet

Interviewing Techniques

Now that you have a potential employee in your office, you must interview them. The interview process is extremely important. This is your way to look for the "right" employee. You need to look for someone that will enhance the spirit of your organization, not someone that could bring it down. You need to decide whether this person has the qualifications that you require, the ability to learn what they may lack, and the personality to work well with others in your company. Consider the following when interviewing:

- Asking the right questions for your purposes.
- NOT asking the wrong questions, legally.
- Asking everything you need to know.
- Asking in such a way as to obtain the most information.
- Asking so as not to offend anyone or violate any laws (city, state, and federal).
- Asking open-ended questions such as:
  - What would your former employer say about you?
  - How would you handle an angry customer?
  - What is your best quality, and why do you think so?
  - What do you want to change about yourself?
  - What do you consider to be your strong points?
  - Why should we hire you?

NOTE: It is normal to interview prospective employees and then call one or two back for a second interview if your decision is a narrow margin between them. After all, you need to make sure you're hiring the right person for the position.

Testing, 1-2-3

Testing of your employees can be done anytime during employment and before promoting to a "higher" position, yet most testing is done BEFORE hiring, for very good reasons. You can test objective skills such as typing, filing, computer skills, and proofreading, and physical abilities such as strength, speed, or being able to reach high shelves. Today's employers require medical, alcohol, and drug tests to further refine their list of applicants.

It is a brilliant move to check Google for prescreening testing facilities in your area. Many of the companies will develop a policy and detailed procedures for your company should a "positive" alcohol/drug test result, along with the proper policy to follow-up on the discovery of such violation. Prescreening should be considered a mechanism of prevention while keeping your company in compliance with federal and state regulations. Develop and stand firm, with a strong intent to maintain and improve safety by reducing the incidences caused by alcohol and drug abuse by employees.

Prescreening should be a pre-employment prerequisite!

Hiring the Capable

Interviewing applicants to find the right employee is no piece of cake. All the guidance and advice anyone can give you will be as nothing if you don't prepare, and understand what your own needs really are.

How much will the person's personality matter? What if a person is perfect for the job, but you can't stand her personality? What if you really love her, but she doesn't grasp the job philosophy? What if she seems to know the work required of her and you love her personality, but wonder if she'll be able to do it satisfactorily because her computer skills are limited? There is yet another possibility: the person who totally understands the job, can do it, and is likable to boot!

So, knowing in advance that you'll be turning down (not hiring) many applicants, develop a gracious way to do so beforehand, to help soften the impact of your decision. Examples: I really love your bubbly personality, Ashley, and if you had the necessary computer skill, you would've been one of my top three choices." "Our company is very small, and often each one of us is called upon to pitch in and help out the other departments. Although you've demonstrated that your accounting skills are above question, Jane, I can see that you are not comfortable answering phones and greeting people. That easy rapport with our customers is a big part of what we stand for. But thank you for your interest in us."

Who Is Capable?

In today's world, most good jobs require a college degree. How wonderful for you, the entrepreneur, that building your own business does not. Yet, now you find yourself in the position of offering one or more good jobs to the public. Who will you hire? Will you now require that college degree of your employees?

Unlike in the past, when you were on the other side of the desk trying to impress your interviewer, YOU are now the interviewer. Remember how you always felt you had so much to offer your would-be employer, but somehow the interview just never got around to bringing it all out in the open? Now's your chance to be the kind of interviewer you always wished you could have had back then.

Sometimes, depending on the personalities involved, the questions about salary create a feeling of awkwardness. Are you planning to pay her less if she tells you her present salary is that much more than what you offer? The answer is probably no. (Remember, you weren't necessarily always paid what you were worth, yet you needed to work. Being underpaid is bad enough without being made to feel that somehow it reflects your worth in the workplace). You know what you are willing and CAN AFFORD to pay. Politely explained, she either can afford to accept the position with the salary or she can turn down the offer. Either way, respect should be given by both the employer and the applicant.

Working Up to the Handbook

Whether you have two or 502 employees, do yourself a gigantic and legally required favor, and create an Employee Handbook! It is a necessity for those who intend to have employees. An Employee Handbook is merely the written form of the company's policies and regulations, compiled and explained in such a way so the employee can understand the philosophy and expectations of the company, and what he or she can expect in return. It should be written clearly, without ambiguities.

The following items cover most of what needs to be addressed; you may discover other items to include for your particular business. Make especially sure that your policies say what you mean, and that you yourself adhere to what they say, because your Handbook may be considered legally binding in the event of a dispute or an unfair employment practice claim.

Labels/Titles/Job Descriptions

Are you more likely to perform up to your potential if someone says, "You'll never be able to do that!" or if they tell you, "Wow! If anybody can do that, it'll be you!"?

Give an employee a low-level label, without much responsibility, and show no confidence in her even doing that well, and what will you have? A mediocre employee, probably suffering from job apathy, and an unrecognized valuable asset—just waiting to be used!

Which would you prefer to be called: Front Desk Secretary, or Special Assistant to the Director? Salesperson, or Account Manager? File Clerk, or Records Coordinator? Titles are free. They cost you nothing, yet they do so much for the person on whom they are conferred. Draw up a list of titles to label the positions you will need filled and see how they "feel." Once the title feels right, be sure the corresponding job description covers everything, so no part of what needs to be done goes unaddressed. Then commit the titles, along with the job descriptions, to paper in order to create the framework for your Employee Handbook.

This brings us to these questions:

- What exactly goes into an Employee Handbook?
- Aren't all equivalent jobs described in pretty much the same way?
- Can anyone just copy some other employer's handbook?

And these answers:

- Your company philosophy. Your view of how your employees fit into the big picture. Their individual job descriptions. Enough additional information to cover every aspect of that which your employees will be a part. (You may want to contact your local SBA office and research their online Employee Handbook, and then have an attorney reform its content so it is suitable for your particular business requirements and needs.) A list of key personnel, pay, benefits, advancement, termination, etc., can be part of the Handbook, or can be put in a separate "Benefits Book."
- Will YOUR saleswomen be just like any ordinary saleswomen, or will they be something far more special?
- You can copy whatever is useful and applicable (since it's not for profit or personal gain), but always remember, the way you word it must reflect YOU.

Employee Bonding

A business can "bond" employees through a licensed bonding company or an insurance company. Basically, this enables an employer to shift the financial responsibility for a specific job or employee to the bonding company.

There is a fee charged and it varies with the type of work. Example: Companies often "bond" workers who enter jobsites and are left unattended while doing their special chores. This takes the financial pressure and worry off the owner while adding insurance to the trustworthiness of the employee. It is also required by some large and technical companies before you can even solicit THEIR business. They want this insurance bonding as part of your initial bid proposal.

Evaluating What's Under Your Nose

Protect yourself first. Determine your applicant's legal right to work in the United States, and fill out an I-9 form when they are hired. Verify what needs to be verified: Green card, driver's license, work permit, sheriff's card, health card, and anything else that may be required in your city, county, or state.

Everything you see and hear is part of the screening process. Do not discount a potential employee's rudeness to "unimportant" people, such as the cleaning or maintenance crew, repairmen, passersby asking for information, etc.

Do not discount your gut feelings; allow everyone the benefit of the doubt, but check those references and contact former employers.

You are not obligated to tell the applicant why you did not select her. However, if your decision is based even slightly on information you discovered in her credit record (if it was necessary to check), you MUST disclose this to her, along with the name and address of the credit agency. The reason for this necessary disclosure is to give her the opportunity to obtain a copy of the same credit report (which will be free, under these circumstances) and check it for errors, which might be holding her back from getting any job.

The right questions will get you the right answers, and the right answers may well get you the right employees.

First Impressions

First impressions can create permanent colors. Observe a person's body language and speech patterns. Nodding, leaning toward you, or copying certain body gestures indicate it's probably a positive impression. Folding arms across body, interrupting, finishing your sentences for you, or crossing legs away from you all indicate more of a negative impression. If it seems you are the one who is not making a good first impression, smile and maintain eye contact. If the first impression cannot be salvaged, perhaps it is better to know right away than to get into business dealings with someone where the "vibrations" are uncomfortable, and you feel less than liked.

Prime Prospects

Do not discount as future employees those who are over a certain age and have retired or for some reason "become available." A side benefit to such an employee is that they usually come with an independent income, and have a rekindled desire to extend their skills and energies into a new environment of work. Tapping into the expanding and diversified talent pool of experienced and mature workers might just ease some internal burdens that you are dealing with and are slowing you down on your journey to achieving your objectives.

The Income Crusade

You're on your own for income potential when you start your own business, but for those who work for you, income is a factor. Generally, the more educated you are, the higher income you seek and expect. Let your would-be employees consider the JOB you offer first, before the salary. When you make it a success, they will benefit as well. It could equally well be their career and the opportunity they are looking for. Offer them a comfortable, happy work environment; constant training to upgrade their knowledge and expertise as required; and incentives such as bonuses, tips, contests, etc., to keep their interest and enthusiasm running high. You might even be looking at future stock options, investment strategies, and/or health insurance as your business grows.

Forward Ho!

It is important to have each employee sign a "non-compete" and "non-disclosure or confidentiality agreement" with your company before signing on. Then, when one of your employees feels the need and desire to branch out on his or her own, don't bother being surprised or upset.

If you are a good example of a successful entrepreneur, it's okay to encourage them and wish them well. I'm not saying it feels good to lose them and the talents they have contributed to your company, but I am saying to keep the friendliness intact because who knows, they may refer a large bit of business or client your way someday. It has happened many times! You may want to ask them to help you find someone to fill their shoes, so to speak, and to stay on long enough to train the new person in all the particulars of that specific job.

Do Employees Know Exactly What It Is They Do?

Have each person describe her job in detail—exactly as she does it. Compare her version of her job with your own job description for that position. You may be surprised.

TIME OUT

Take time to work...it is the price of success

Take time to think...it is the source of power

Take time to play...it is the secret of youth

Take time to read...it is the foundation of wisdom

Take time to be friendly...it is the road to happiness

Take time to dream...it is hitching your wagon to a star

Take time to love...it is the highest joy of life

Take time to laugh...it is the music of the soul

Employees' Needs
When Your Employees Decide to Leave

Employees tend to look out for themselves—and rightfully so. If your employer-employee relationship has been open, honest, and friendly, not to worry. If your employee is feeling that she needs to get all she can out of the job before she leaves, you may need to sit up and pay attention, and evaluate if she is even needed for a two weeks' notice.

This is where those employment law lawyers sometimes come in. If there is a way around something, or a way to get you to make her departure more lucrative, they'll find it. Avoid the 'What can I take?—What can you give?' game by being clear up-front regarding this issue.

Because of the nature of people to look out for themselves, employers are being ever so cautious with their application and interviewing process. Many companies have their lawyers draw up their policy manuals, and the language used reflects that "us vs. them" stance. Some examples:

- Additional paperwork necessary for employment shall include any agreement entered into with the employee, any and all licensing or legal authorization necessary (i.e., registrations, identification cards, work permits, and other, as required by law), and any and all commission and bonus schedules.

- No employee shall have any express or implied contract or any other rights to employment and any intention to create such rights is expressly disclaimed. All employment is "at will" and may be

LADIES START YOUR BUSINESS

terminated by the company without
cause in its sole discretion.

While this "looking out for number one" position
is taken on both sides of the employment equation, and
lawyers are paid big bucks to legally tie up loose ends and
check on all the "shalls" and "shall nots," if an employee
is determined to make an issue of something, she will.
Whether or not she'll have a legal leg to stand on in
court will not keep her from walking all over you. The
bottom line in this department is that if you approach
your employees as though you truly care about them
and value them, you will more often than not cultivate in
them a genuine reciprocal attitude of caring about you
and the work they do.

The Dearly Departing

There are some considerations that you should
entertain before, to save aggravation after the fact:

- Severance pay is probably the most
  common benefit you can offer
  departing employees, but should
  you? Shouldn't you? Must you?
  You're not required by law to do so if
  you had to fire them, or let them go
  for your own reasons (such as going
  out of business). Always check the
  law regarding the "musts," but do
  what you can regarding how you feel
  about the dearly departing.
- If your employee participated in a

stock option plan, you could offer her cash in lieu of her exercising her option, if the subject comes up. The terms should be expressed in the "When Employees Leave" section of the Employee Handbook.

- Sometimes the things that have no cost have the most value. If you hold the employee in high regard, and even your independent contractors have nothing but praise for her work, put it in writing. Be kind enough to collect all the praise for her performance over the many months or years she was with you, and present it to her as she departs. (You will, of course, keep the originals for your own files.)

- Understand why she's leaving. Don't let her drift away with memories or misconceptions of what went wrong or why. Chances are, you've been on top of things, and never let little disagreements or differences escalate into volcanic eruptions, so there should be no good-bye surprises.

- Be very clear in the Employee Handbook about what belongs to whom—legally, morally, and of course physically. It is very easy for an employee to feel so attached to a client, or a discovery, or to some physical item that was exclusively "hers" while at work, that she does not think clearly when it is time to go. Some things, if taken, leave no gaping wound; other things, when missing, could sabotage your business.

- Don't burn your bridges. True, she's leaving you, yet her next adventure may not work out and she would give anything to have you ask her back. If the parting remains pleasant, she won't be hesitant to offer you her services again. And you won't be reluctant to accept, providing her shoes have not been filled.

Special Employee Benefits

There are many types of special employee benefits you can offer that will greatly improve things for your employees and increase their longevity with your business. Remember, you have to balance costs versus productivity. Training a new employee every month can take up a lot of your time and efforts, and cost quite a bit of money, depending on the training. The work environment must be a place where the employee feels comfortable and secure. At the same time, you must compete in the marketplace and additional expenses drive up your costs. Consider the following possible added benefits:

For Health and Comfort:

1. Annual flu shots
2. Alternate work plan for sick days
3. Smoke-free environment or filtered air

For Health and Convenience:

1. Optional work plan for inclement weather
2. Transportation, if needed
3. Hot and cold beverages
4. Exercise and rest area
5. Bottled or filtered water

Little Extra Considerations:

1. Company incentives for good ideas, safety, saving the business money, etc.
2. Flex-time, job-sharing, adjustable hours
3. Tickets to events, media giveaways, parties, seminars, conventions, motivation-related courses, training to better her skills
4. Employee Newsletter: offer open participation and perhaps it can be a forum for employees' talents

Best of all, you can offer a happy, dedicated, optimistic atmosphere in which to work; one in which you genuinely care about your employees and hope they will stay on with you as you grow and prosper, enabling you to share your prosperity with them.

God in the Workplace: Okay? Not Okay? Legal?

God. It's one of those words. You know the kind: words that mean different things to different people; words that sometimes offend others when they hear them spoken. So, what's a businessperson to do? Can we go around policing everyone's words, and check the context in which they are spoken? I think not. Can we draw up a policy that forbids this and that, and allows the other things? I think not. Can we punish people for using "trigger" or "provocative" words that send some people into a fit or a frenzy? You know the answer. Can we have a caring and considerate office policy that clearly states our stand on how we deal with situations covering religion, religion-related activities, and religious-sounding words in the workplace? Yes, I believe we can.

When we use the term "office policy," does that cover what goes on in the physical office only, or in any area connected to or associated with the office, such as the bathroom, the hallways, the lunchroom, the grounds, the warehouse, etc.? And does it include what one does during lunchtime and breaks, or only working hours?

It is truly amazing how far we've come in some ways regarding employer-employee relations, and how stilted our progress has been in others. We have become, as a generality, a nation of complainers rather than a nation of community players. What you, as a businesswoman, need to know is that those you come in contact with will have different feelings about, and philosophies regarding, what is appropriate or acceptable in your workplace. In particular, this issue will impact you personally when it comes to your employees, and their interpretation of the Civil Rights Act and the power of the Employees Equal Opportunities Commission. If you do not know your employees well enough before hiring, or learn enough about them during the pre-hiring interview phase, you may find yourself in for an unhappy surprise when one of them makes an issue out of your saying "Thank God" when the bank calls to tell you that your line of credit has been approved, and it sends you to court.

Religion IS an issue. There are more than 200 officially recognized religious sects in this country, and more than 1,000 unconventional "non-recognized" groups. Each one has adherents who wouldn't be affiliated with their group if they didn't "feel" something about it, or believe in it. To "step" on their beliefs and their feelings is like someone attacking a mother's child. You don't do it and get away without an emotional battle. This is an issue of the heart and soul. This is a spiritual thing; you cannot fight it with logic, common sense, or consensus. It is ALWAYS, 100 percent of the time, better to deal with it before it becomes an emotional issue, rather than after.

Because you cannot ask about their religion on the application, or bring up their religious beliefs or practices in the interview, you must find a way to get an indication (other than your out-and-out gut feeling) of how would-be employees might react to something you normally say or do, or something your company would normally be involved in or associated with. You might say something like, "Because many of our customers bring their children to our place of business, we like to decorate for the various holidays. We put up such things as Valentine hearts, Easter bunnies, shamrocks, Thanksgiving turkeys, and Santa Clauses or nativities. Would that in any way bother you or interfere with your doing your job?"

If the answer is no, you could add, "We also have a company philosophy that reflects caring about each other's sensitivities, since we know that all people who work together don't think alike about everything in their personal lives. For instance, if I wore a message button to work that proclaimed 'pro-choice,' and you happen to believe that by wearing that button and believing that message I am advocating murder, I would be stepping on your sensitivities, showing little regard for your heartfelt beliefs. We would then be in the position of forcing our version of our 'rights' on each other; mine to wear the button, and yours to not be offended or harassed by such an affront to your beliefs. Rather than subject ourselves to that kind of unpleasantness and work disruption derived from emotional upheaval, our policy is that rather than offend, even unknowingly, each other and our customers—on whom we depend for our living—we request that personal messages not be worn on clothing where they can be seen. If you feel the need to wear something because of a commitment or a vow, simply keep it out of common view during the work hours; you may display it during your breaks away from your work area and lunchtimes, and of course after work hours are over. Since everyone who works for this company must agree to be considerate of the others who work here, as well as of our customers, do you anticipate any difficulty with that policy?"

If the answer is no (be sure and have a signed copy of such a policy after hiring), you could go on. "Obviously, in keeping with that policy of considerateness, we like to know when there is anything special that we can do to avoid placing our employees in the position of feeling uncomfortable, uncared about, or not accommodated in one of their needs. All we ask, out of consideration for our position, is to be told about the need for the accommodation in advance so that we may have time to make the necessary accommodation. Does that policy sound agreeable to you?" It's hard to imagine how you could be any fairer, more caring, more conscientious, or more tuned in to the legal ramifications of on-the-job complications. Yet, people being who and what they are, there may be and will be any number of variations on the theme of employee complaints.

It is advisable that you have an attorney draw up your legal "ancillary" documents, in addition to the Employee Handbook, and have the employee sign each document as it is explained.

Familiarize yourself with the wording, intention, and "spirit" of the law regarding such matters. Every one of us who enjoys the freedoms of this country does so because they are granted to all.

The personal part of all this is that employees are not obligated to work in a workplace that offends them, nor are we obligated to choose employees who will upset and undermine our business. In fact, the law states that an employee's beliefs cannot cause undue hardship to his or her employer.

Remember, however, that your company and workplace did not come into existence for the sake of giving your employees a stage to display or discuss their individual religious or personal beliefs.

In your quest to establish and maintain peace and harmony in the workplace, remember: You can tease all of the people some of the time, and some of the people all of the time, but you cannot possibly please all of the people you tease! And some people have absolutely no sense of humor when it comes to THEIR religion.

There's No Sense in Being "The Boss" If You Can't Show It; Or, How to Create Poor Morale in the Workplace

A bad boss is an easy thing to become. Please don't become one. Employees perform at their best when they respect their boss. Please don't do the following:

- Talk about the high cost of everything, and how hard it is for you to make a profit.
- Talk about the importance of having a nice office, impressive furniture, or an expensive and impressive car that reflects your title as owner; in other words—bragging.
- Expect everything; and give only what you have to.
- Act your part: you're the BOSS, they're only the hired hands.
- Set the tone: you're all there to work. They can be happy on their own time.

- Only see that profits are king! Anything that interferes with making as much money as possible needs to be eliminated, even if it means firing people for making what they think are little mistakes.
- Think benefits are for BIG business. If your employees want more than their paychecks, they can go somewhere else.
- Refuse to ask for anyone's opinion and ignore suggestions. You can run your business without your employees' concurrence or advice.
- Remember: the best part of being BOSS means never having to say you're sorry.

Try and create a familiar mind-set that says: I am aware of how I come across to my employees/coworkers/customers, and I will endeavor to refrain from acting egotistical and being dominating, manipulative, or controlling toward them. Nothing I want, hope for, or work for will become an addiction to me. Don't expect less of your work team than they are capable of giving. And remind them often of your confidence in their ability.

Managing Older Employees—How Old Is Older?

Most of what management does is more or less standard, no matter who you are "managing." Yet, there are some considerations one might have for older employees. If you're thirty-ish, older is forty-ish and up. If you're forty-ish, older is fifty-ish. If you're fifty-ish, you may already be older.

So, what's the difference between younger and older employees anyway? (What's the difference between you and your children, or between you and the younger generation?) Depending on which category of older they are in, older workers generally appreciate their jobs more and take their responsibilities more seriously. Older workers generally feel it more when they make mistakes and may start to feel inadequate on the job. Older workers are closer to retirement age, and may have more reason to stick with it for the duration. Older workers usually understand the work ethic, and they understand authority. However, they also know when they've done a really great job and nobody bothered to mention it, let alone thank them.

No matter how close in age you are to your work team, and no matter how you perceive them, remember: every individual worker has her own concerns, and her own way of viewing management. If the way you deal with your four employees makes three of them happy, don't assume the fourth employee is the odd one out. She might be operating from a different standpoint.

Office Praise: How to Bestow It to Everyone's Advantage

- ALWAYS BE GENUINE. Fake praise or glad-handing spoils it for the real thing.

- Never praise one at the expense of another, or others. "I wish everyone was more like you" is not recommended. Not only does it lower others' self-esteem, it's bound to put the one being praised in an uncomfortable position with her coworkers.
- Surprise! As with criticism, praise in private. Some days we're worthy of praise; some days we're not. Why should everyone have to know everyone else's up and down days?
- Praise works better if you also know how to criticize correctly. Example: If you're used to saying, "You always get the message wrong!" and the person on the receiving end knows that she gets it right most of the time, a better way to phrase it might be, "I really feel frustrated when I have to act on information that is not correct." Instead of saying, "I'm always so proud of you" and it not meaning a thing, lend more impact by saying, "I feel so proud of our company when I see the way you handle the customers."
- Praise the things that matter to the person being praised.
  - Neatness, to the neatnik

- - Customer management, to the conscientious public relations or salesperson
  - Saving the company money, time, or effort, to the efficient and organized person
- Be specific; not "Good job!" or "That was well done!"
- Be brief. Don't make little things into big deals.
- Be brief OFTEN, so that when you want to elaborate, it will be listened to and believed, and "felt" as having value.
- Keep notes. Jot down the things you praise employees for on a daily basis (there may be days your notepad remains blank) and refine the list at the end of the week. Add this information to their personnel files on a monthly basis. Your notes could look like this:

Monday:	Paula saved the Shelby account.
	Becky worked until 7:00 p.m. to finish the "Little Angels" project
Thurs.:	Patty finally learned the computer
Friday:	Betty made everyone muffins
Sat.:	Wes came in to fix the vacuum

Paula:	Efficient, clever, good with people
Becky:	Does what it takes to get a job done
Tenny:	Always willing to learn new things
Sarah:	Thoughtful, team-oriented
Ryan:	Goes above and beyond what is required of him

Mistake Management—In Advance

On written matter: proofreed, prooffread, proofrede. There should be no excuse at all for obvious mistakes on business cards, even if they have been okayed by you. Train everyone in your workplace to call anything to your attention that doesn't seem right, and to correct obvious mistakes without your okay. Example: An obvious mistake would be if, instead of your company name reading Prunella's Party Pies, it read Prune Ella's Part Tea Pies.

Warding off mistakes in advance is preferable to any amount of "fixing" them after the fact. Be realistic, sensitive to the circumstances, and caring. Cultivate some conscientious comments to keep the mistake-maker from thinking she sank the Titanic. Try one of these:

- It's okay; you didn't just stand there, you tried to do something.
- It's not the end of the world, but we can see it from here! Oops! We all make mistakes.

- You'll know what to watch out for next time.
- That's one mistake none of us will ever make again.

If it was your mistake, apologize if necessary, look for the lesson in it, find the better or correct way to do it, and then fix it. Don't cover it up or pretend it didn't happen. Above all, don't view yourself as a failure, and don't give up!

Acceptable or Unacceptable: Decide in Advance

Remember, you are the boss and therefore you must make the decisions. There are a host of things that employees will do if you let them, and you need to decide if you will tolerate them. Things such as:

- Sitting on desks or tables
- Putting feet on desks or other furniture (street grime on chair seats is a BIG no-no for me)
- Food spread out on desks
- Smoking in front of your place of business where customers come in and out
- Careless posture (imagine the worst)
- Using someone else's desk/chair/ workspace without asking
- Rummaging through another's desk/ drawers/files (I don't think so!)

- Leaving wrappers, cups, junk mail, or refuse in or near another's area
- NOT DOING what needs to be done, regardless of whose "job" it is:
  - Emptying filled wastebaskets
  - Replacing toilet tissue roll and hand towels
  - Dusting noticeably dusty areas
  - Picking up things from the floor
  - Wiping up spills
  - Vacuuming dirty carpets
  - Tidying up the reception area/ offices

Things You Never Liked in Other People, and Don't Want to See in Your Employees

We all remember some clerk in a store talking to her friend instead of waiting on us. You knew that if you were her boss, you would give her a "talking-to." Now you are the boss, and you need to look for those things that you wouldn't like to see, such as:

- Unhelpfulness, which translates into giving only the absolute minimum amount of information or assistance asked for.
- Not acknowledging a customer who enters the business.
- Robot-like demeanor, which shows itself in a frozen face, glassy eyes, mechanical movements, an

inability to think for itself, and preprogrammed, short and snippy answers.

- Canned messages and responses, which don't even allow for an original "You have a point there" or "Of course I'll explain that to you." Heaven forbid there should be any humor involved—it might require a soundtrack.

- Witch-like faces, which can be seen only in conjunction with witch-like personalities. Cleverly cultivated to ward off any but the most pressing of questions or comments. Can be found in areas where you tend to need help the most.

- Age jealousy, or age snobbery. So you're young, and heading for your success a lot sooner than the person who has to wait on you. Is that any reason for her to practically throw the documents at you? So you're a lot older than the person who has to wait on you. Can you practically hear her snickering at someone as "old" as you daring to try something new?

- Making what you have to do more complicated or time-consuming, because the people you have to deal with don't care. If there were such a thing as a simple sign stating "This office does not make copies," it might deprive the clerks of seeing the look on your face when they tell you that you need those copies before they can grant you the permit, after you just spent twenty minutes in line, fifteen minutes going over your application at the window, and the last hour looking forward to finally going home after a hectic day of waiting in lines.

Contents of a Detailed Employee Handbook

There is no "one size fits all" when it comes to an Employee Handbook. I'm including this brief outline as a guide to build upon. It helps to be aware of what, exactly, an Employee Handbook has in its contents. What are you looking for and where do you begin? Start with this prototype and customize yours to suit your business. Like I always say, make sure to run your Handbook by an attorney for a double-check!

1. **An equal opportunity statement**
State that an employee's religion, age, sex, national origin, race, or color will have nothing to do with hiring, promotion, pay, or benefits.

2. **Physical examinations and testing**
Establish your right to conduct both pre- and post-employment physicals, as well as alcohol and drug testing,

at company expense. The intent is to improve and maintain a safe work place and to comply with federal and state regulations. Keep your examinations nondiscriminatory; i.e., not just for women, older people, ethnic groups, etc.

3. Probationary period

State the period during which a new employee can be dismissed without a hearing on the cause (usually thirty, sixty, or ninety days). Also state when benefits start to accrue.

4. Work hours

Define the work week and the time allowed for breaks and lunch. State the cut-off time for each pay period.

5. Employee status

Define the nature of each type of employee: full-time, part-time, temporary, "exempt," and "nonexempt." State clearly what benefits each is eligible for. You must keep some sort of documented record for hours worked by nonexempt employees. Early sign-ins or late sign-outs will make you liable for overtime pay in case of a conflict or dispute.

6. Overtime pay

State clearly whether overtime is paid for work over forty hours each week, or over eight hours on a given day, and how much is paid for working on a holiday. Clearly state that pay for overtime must be approved by a supervisor.

7. Absence and lateness

State that frequent or unexplained absence from work, or tardiness in reporting to work, will be considered just cause for disciplinary action. The employees' regular attendance on the job is vital to the operation.

8. Severance pay

This is based on seniority. Generally, the scale is a week's pay for less than three years tenure, two weeks' pay for up to six years, three weeks' pay from six to ten years, etc. Exclude employees who are released for cause. You may also exclude employees who leave voluntarily.

9. Performance review with salary increases

Review wages periodically during the year: quarterly, semi-annually, or on the anniversary of employment.

10. Time clock or sign-in system

The company policy should prohibit employees from both recording another employee's time and failing to record their own.

11. Emergency shutdown time

State if company policy allows for reduced or regular "call-in" wages if there is reason for your business to be closed, such as due to bad weather, or some other just cause. Then state up to how long this could be in effect, and how much advance notice, if possible, will be given.

12. Group insurance benefits

State general coverage, what portion of the premium costs the company will pay, how long a new employee must wait to receive coverage, and if there is a conversion privilege for continuing the coverage for a stated time after the employee leaves the job (COBRA).

13. Holidays

List all holidays that are observed by the company, how long an employee has to work to qualify for a paid holiday, what happens if the holiday occurs during an employee's vacation, and what pay is given for work on the holiday. Be sure to state that employees have the right to take religious holidays without pay.

14. Vacations

Consult your local Bureau of Labor statistics surveys and other published information regarding local practices. State how a new employee qualifies for vacation time, and if a person may choose to work instead of taking a vacation. State if accrued vacation pay will be given at severance, and if a person on leave of absence will accrue vacation time.

15. Personal time and sick leave

Ten to fifteen days per year is reasonable to allow an employee, but the number is subject to flexibility, depending on your particular company and number of employees. You might design a payback system for those employees who do not abuse the privilege. If you choose to pay for time off only in the case of illness, state if you require "proof of illness" and what will be accepted as such.

16. Disability leave of absence

Federal law requires leave time for disability due to pregnancy to be equal to that allowed for disabilities that affect only males. You must set some reasonable time limit during which you will guarantee job protection for a disabled worker. A sixty- to ninety-day grace period is typical. You may require pregnant women to sign statements of intent to return to work, provided you require male workers disabled for other reasons to do the same. You may also reserve the right to require a physical examination by a company-appointed doctor, if required, of both males and females.

17. **Military leave of absence**
This is required under federal law for National Guard or Reserve service. State that a copy of the orders for the military duty requiring leave be filed with the employee's supervisor. NOTE: Employees may not be compelled to use vacation or personal time for military leave, and the job must be held open for the returning employee. Employees must not be discriminated against in pay, promotions, or job assignments due to such military affiliation.

18. **Personal leave of absence**
If you should decide to grant such leaves, you may want to specify that they may not exceed thirty or sixty

days, and that they may not be taken to look for or perform another job, or to start another business.

19. Jury duty

This is required by law; some local statues also require you to pay all or a portion of the employee's wages. Depending on those local laws, you may want to set limits on how many days of jury duty you'll pay for, and set a qualifying period of employment before you'll pay for jury leave. If you pay the employee a partial amount, as required by local statues, pay them the difference between the amount of their jury duty check and the pay they would have received at their job.

20. Bereavement pay

Employees expect a company to be very lenient in this matter, and rightfully so, especially in the event of a death in their immediate family. Typically, company policy should allow for three to five days off with pay. You might want to specify what "immediate family" means, as well.

21. Cause for discipline

Some industries—most often those employing unskilled or semiskilled workers—believe that a list of "shop rules" is essential. If you post them, these rules must be as comprehensive as possible, nondiscriminatory, and phrased in such a way that you're not "forced" to dismiss a good employee for an unintentional infraction.

22. Complaints and grievances

There should be some basis for appeal in the event an employee feels a supervisor's policies are unjust, as long as you do not create an avenue whereby employees can bypass their supervisors. Rather, encourage employees to talk things over with their supervisors first, to avoid workplace dissension or chaos.

Mechanics of the Handbook

- Place typed pages back to back inside plastic sheet protectors (the kind with holes for use in a three-ring binder).
- Title the book—or books—in large, easy-to-read letters:
  EMPLOYEE HANDBOOK
  JOB DESCRIPTIONS
  BENEFITS BOOK
  COMPANY POLICY MANUAL
  OPERATIONS MANUAL

- You can put all your information in one binder, with dividers, or use separate ones.
- Place binder in a common area for employees; i.e., within the personnel office
- Update information as it legally changes—as soon as possible. File old information for at least six months.

Employ-Ease

Discipline

Discipline should come only after you have tried to counsel the employee. The proper course of action then is a general warning, to a verbal warning, to a written warning, to dismissal.

The counseling meeting

This is between the employee and her supervisor, with another person (witness) present. The supervisor will try to resolve the problem. Notes are taken regarding the issue(s) discussed, and all parties present sign and date the paper, which is then placed in the employee's file.

Official company reprimand

This is for problems unresolved with the above procedure. This is formal discipline, written up on preprinted reprimand forms and signed and dated by all parties present. A copy may be given to the employee; other copies are retained in the employee's file.

All Handbooks and Job Descriptions Are Not Created Equal

As you may already know, in an Employee Handbook it's not just what you say, it's the way you say it. Consider using caring, detailed, creative, and team-centered ways while informing your employees of the company's policies. Good luck with your manual; it will be one of the most vital tools your company will have when you arrive at the stage of needing employees. Research and research again before finalizing it.

A LAST WORD

> *Experience isn't an accident, it's a reward that's given to people who pursue it. That's a deliberate act, and it's hard work.*
> -Paul Theroux, Mosquito Coast

You've read this book and have decided you're committed. Don't let the "creeping delay bug" interfere with your forward motion or enthusiasm, and above all keep the notion and idea alive that "you want what is yours." Maybe what you want is to believe in yourself so you can soar with newfound confidence into the world of business. Once empowered with knowledge and the where-to-go-get-it kind of help provided in this book, you can and will become a force for lasting change in this world, in one way or another. I believe in you!

There are approximately eleven million women entrepreneurs in America. Yet, you are solely in charge of your destiny, so it's important that you create a vision of where you want to go, how high you want to set your goals, and (perhaps most important) why you want it. Keeping your vision focused makes your mission easier. Business is many different things to many different women. Success and failure are on the same continuum if you think about them in regard to individuals. For instance, what might be one woman's level of success might be another's failure. Never measure your own personal level of achievement against someone else's success level, or even listen to another's fixed opinions on what "actual" success is.

After you have collected all your facts and sifted and inspected them, is it natural to reach a conclusion—your own personal conclusion. Material and monetary items are important and necessary for surviving in life, but they are secondary when it comes to being happy and content with what you are doing with your life. Seek what is in your heart, what it truly is that you want, and then speak from your heart. Do good unto others, and don't forget to help those who need help when you're a thriving businesswoman.

It's a small world. It would be a shame to miss it while we're here. Sounds like something from a storybook, right? Well, this is one fairy tale what won't end at the stroke of midnight. It's your dream, so…Dream Deep and Think Big!

Made in the USA